# From Your Friend, Carey Dean

# From Your Friend, Carey Dean

*Letters from Nebraska's Death Row*

LISA KNOPP

CASCADE Books • Eugene, Oregon

FROM YOUR FRIEND, CAREY DEAN
Letters from Nebraska's Death Row

Copyright © 2022 Lisa Knopp. All rights reserved. Except for brief quotations in critical publications or reviews, no part of this book may be reproduced in any manner without prior written permission from the publisher. Write: Permissions, Wipf and Stock Publishers, 199 W. 8th Ave., Suite 3, Eugene, OR 97401.

Cascade Books
An Imprint of Wipf and Stock Publishers
199 W. 8th Ave., Suite 3
Eugene, OR 97401

www.wipfandstock.com

PAPERBACK ISBN: 978-1-6667-0787-8
HARDCOVER ISBN: 978-1-6667-0788-5
EBOOK ISBN: 978-1-6667-0789-2

*Cataloguing-in-Publication data:*

Names: Knopp, Lisa, author.

Title: From your friend, Carey Dean: letters from Nebraska's death row / Lisa Knopp.

Description: Eugene, OR: Cascade Books, 2022 | Includes bibliographical references.

Identifiers: ISBN 978-1-6667-0787-8 (paperback) | ISBN 978-1-6667-0788-5 (hardcover) | ISBN 978-1-6667-0789-2 (ebook)

Subjects: LCSH: Christianity and justice. | Criminal justice, Administration of—United States. | Church work with prisoners.

Classification: BS680.J8 K50 2022 (paperback) | BS680 (ebook)

05/09/22

# Contents

| | | |
|---|---|---|
| *Preface* | | vii |
| *Prologue* | | xiii |
| 1 | The Challenge | 1 |
| 2 | The Early Years | 9 |
| 3 | The Rest of the Story | 23 |
| 4 | "What Is Death Row Like?" | 35 |
| 5 | Whispers and Shouts | 49 |
| 6 | "A Part of Me Wants to Live but Most of Me Does Not" | 61 |
| 7 | Behind the Headlines | 77 |
| 8 | "Just Call Me Dr.-Want-to-Be-Phil" | 92 |
| 9 | "Waiting for Some Sort of Outcome" | 104 |
| 10 | The Outcome | 116 |
| *Afterword from Carey Dean Moore* | | 135 |
| *Acknowledgments* | | 137 |
| *Works Cited and Consulted* | | 139 |

# Preface

A cardboard box that once held reams of paper sits atop a two-drawer file cabinet in my home office. It is jammed with twenty-three manila envelopes standing on end. Some are bulging: the edges of smaller, white envelopes jut from the top. A few are almost flat. On each, I've written a year (1995 through 2018) and jotted brief notes about the contents. These are the 320 letters that my late friend, Carey Dean Moore, inmate #32947 on Nebraska's death row from 1980 to 2018, wrote to me during the twenty-three-year span of our friendship. From April 2018 to May 2019, I spent part of most days rereading the letters and quoting from them as I drafted this book.

The book that resulted is, above all, the story of an extraordinary friendship, carried on primarily through letters between two people whose paths probably wouldn't have crossed if one hadn't been on death row and the other a death penalty abolitionist. But this book has two more stories to tell: that of our nation's badly broken penal system and the spiritual connection between me and a double murderer who was transformed through his relationship with God. As a writer, I'm humbled and overwhelmed by the enormity of doing justice to any one of these strands, much less all three at once.

I kept all of the letters that Carey sent me because they were so personal and inspiring and because they chronicled my life as well as that of my friend. It would have been wrong to throw them away. Although Carey turned down my offer to coauthor this book, he gave me his blessings on the project, promising to provide any information I needed and granting permission for me to quote anything he'd written to me. "Whatever you wanted to quote of me (which would be 100% fine), I simply need to read and approve first [. . .]—but I'll do my extreme best not to change any thing that I've written to you [. . .] Of course I trust you, Lisa" (May 18, 2018). When I read that last line, I was deeply moved and stricken with self-doubt: Carey trusted *me* to get his story right. That would have been more easily achieved if he were alive, reading and commenting on what I'd written, filling in gaps and striking out passages. But he was executed, and even though I had freer rein to tell the story, I had less confidence in my reporting and reflecting.

I don't present my view of my friend as right or definitive. I've excerpted from the letters what I consider to be the most pertinent or illustrative passages, which is a subjective process. Had I chosen different excerpts, the result would have been a different characterization, a different book. I could have written a book focused on the childhood influences that created a murderer. I could have written a true crime book in the spirit of Truman Capote's *In Cold Blood* or Vincent Bugliosi's *Helter Skelter*, using the letters only for research. But the book that I wanted to write was one that told the story of a man awaiting execution and the conditions in which he lived, and of the remarkable and unlikely friendship that he and I enjoyed. With some aspects of Carey's life, I was challenged by my desire to faithfully represent him while appealing to a diverse readership—death penalty abolitionists and supporters, Christians, non-Christians, Nebraskans who wanted the story behind a man who'd been executed in their state, people interested in stories about friendship. For instance, I wrestled with how much space to devote to his Christianity, as it not only provided what were for him engaging and defining metaphors but the grand narrative of his life. Indeed, more than anything else, his relationship with God guided his thoughts and actions. Yet some readers don't understand or are put off by Christian spirituality. So, in some passages, I've preserved Carey's characteristic move from the mundane into the spiritual; but in others, I've cut short the latter. I've also cut over half of the many exclamations ("Praise the Lord!"; "Alleluyah!") and the emojis that concluded many of his paragraphs.

Writing about others gives me pause, as it can change a relationship, sometimes for the better and sometimes for the worse. In the thirty-odd years that I've been writing creative nonfiction, I've found that whether I am describing the quotidian in my subject's everyday life or reflecting on the nature of our relationship, differences of opinion are inevitable, not only about the meaning of the facts but about the facts themselves. And, too, writing about the life of another is always an act of appropriation, of claiming someone else's story as one's own. The only antidote I know to the hazards of writing about another is honesty, humility, and prayer.

I was reluctant to write about others currently on death row, as I didn't want to inadvertently harm anyone or disrespect anyone's privacy. Carey and I agreed that if he was still alive when I finished the book, he would let me know if he approved of what I'd written about the people he lived with. But in his absence, I would, for the most part, limit myself to writing about those inmates who had been executed or who had passed away from illness or suicide. If I mentioned a living inmate, I would do so in a factual, neutral sense, like naming a person he ate meals with, or else rely on what Carey said about him in writing. Carey urged me to write about his dear friend, the late Arthur Gales, whom he believed to be innocent. So, I have named Art and have repeated some of what Carey said about Art's case and their friendship.

Carey was quite frank about the abuse that he suffered as a child. Yet, I felt uncomfortable writing about the Moore family. To name his family members in a published book was to draw attention to them that they might not want. But Carey mentioned them often, and they were a critical part of his story. Finding the right balance between revealing enough of what he told me about his background that readers could understand the formative influences in his life without bringing unwanted attention to his family members and friends was challenging. I chose not to include the majority of the illustrative stories that Carey told me in person and through letters. As much as possible, I have omitted the names of family members and friends. While Carey wrote often about his brother, Donald, and while I saved letters that Donald wrote to me, anything I've written about him either comes from newspaper articles or trial transcripts—public documents. Likewise, for information about the families of Reuel Van Ness Jr. and Maynard Helgeland, the two men that Carey murdered, I relied on articles from the Omaha and Lincoln newspapers and news clips from their television stations. Carey sent me letters that he had received from some of the victims' family members. While this gave me insight into how they felt about Carey and how the murders continued to affect them, I haven't included anything from those letters.

I present the workings of Nebraska's correctional and legal systems largely from Carey's perspective. But I've also provided what I felt was essential background, context, or interpretation. Because I believe that people who commit crimes should serve just, fair sentences in safe, humane institutions, I am profoundly troubled by some of what I know about the workings of the criminal justice system in Nebraska and the United States. My opinions about this are woven into the story of my and Carey's friendship.

Letter writers tend to tell anecdotes about the distant past as well-constructed stories, complete with a narrative arc, clear connections, and meaning. But they tend to present events that are in the midst of unfolding in fragments, episodes, or installments that may extend over a few or several or many dozens of letters before resolving. As I reread Carey's letters, I watched the development of many stories, the ends of which neither he nor I knew at the time he wrote of them, such as his introduction to and development of a relationship with a brother, Bartley Joseph or John, who was adopted out of the Moore family as a baby and found his way back to it decades later; Carey's search for his daughter; his struggles to create and maintain the death row Bible study; his almost constant yearning to stop his appeals and to volunteer for execution. Initially, I'd intended to write a chronological narrative about our friendship. But as John McPhee observes, when crafting creative nonfiction, the author often feels "considerable tension" between chronology and theme. "The narrative wants to move from point to point through time, while topics that have arisen now and again across someone's life cry out to be collected." I gave in to both impulses. The events that led up to my first visit with death row inmates, meeting Carey, and learning about his early life and the murders were best dealt with chronologically, while persistent or recurring themes and issues, such as Carey's spiritual life, his service to others, and his refusal to fight his execution, "cr[ied] out" to be dealt with thematically. What resulted is a book that contains elements of both a memoir and a collection of essays.

I'd had no intention of writing a book about my friend until the last several months of his life, so it never occurred to me to follow up on some of the subjects that he had written about, either in face-to-face conversations or in my return letters. But that's the way it is with personal correspondence. If he'd written about four or five topics in one of his letters, I might respond to but a few of those items and devote the rest of my letter to what was going on in my life. Carey did the same when answering my letters. When I drafted the book, I encountered many instances when it seems I should have known something that I didn't. When he was in solitary confinement, did he have his Bible with him or not? What became of the correctional officer who Carey said had "poisoned" the water jugs that the men on death row drank from? During his last few months, Carey answered my questions until we ran out of time.

To fill in the gaps, I could have interviewed his friends, family, attorneys, pastors, fellow inmates, Nebraska Department of Correctional Services employees, the children of the men he murdered, and other correspondents. I read some but not most of the court transcripts. I could have read the letters that Carey sent to Dave, his twin brother, which Dave generously offered me access to. But I didn't. I was overwhelmed by the thought of doing justice to the 320 letters that I'd saved. So, I stayed in the box atop the file cabinet, drawing the information I needed from the letters that Carey wrote to me, which proved to be a limiting, yet liberating parameter. For instance, when I heard about a concern that Carey had raised in the death row Bible study on a day when I wasn't there, I felt that I should inquire and write about that, too. Then I remembered: stay in the box. When there's something I don't or can't know through the letters, I say so.

During the last three months of Carey's life, when we knew that he would not fight his pending execution, I wrote fast drafts—sketches, really—of nine chapters of the book so that I could present, for his scrutiny, an annotated table of contents. He weighed in on the titles, on what I proposed to cover in each chapter. And he advised me on how to approach the material: "If there's anything juicy you might like to write about it, just ask . . . It can't hurt. You should write about 'some' sensitive areas from both of us, which should keep readers interested and some comical or funny things [. . .]. What do you think?" (June 20, 2018).

Early in the writing process, I realized that I couldn't just tell Carey's story. Because our letters chronicle the story of a friendship, I had to include myself. Consequently, the book had to be a blend of biography and memoir, with the balance weighted more toward the former than the latter. For the most part, I expose myself in order to reveal my subject or our friendship. I kept copies of fewer than 20 percent of the letters that I wrote to Carey, so it was challenging to know what to say about myself. Fortunately, before Carey responded to my letters, he quoted a sentence or two of mine so that I'd remember what I'd written to him. This helped me recall "who I was" at different points in our long friendship.

I have not edited the letters or condensed them for clarity, except to correct typos or to restore a dropped letter or a forgotten closing quotation mark. I have marked misspellings with "[sic]." Carey used three dots to pace his prose or create emphasis. When I've deleted words from an excerpt, I've noted that choice with ellipses within brackets—[. . .]—to distinguish my omissions from his stylistic choice.

I went into this project not knowing if my subject would be dead or alive when I wrote the last page. Though Carey and I knew that an execution would have provided the tidiest ending, I assured him that he didn't have to die for me to finish the book. To end with him, a sixty-year-old man who'd spent thirty-eight years on death row, watching as yet another execution date came and went, is an ending that would have represented his life as long as I'd known him, as well as the circumstances of others in Nebraska and beyond awaiting the fulfillment or commutation of their death sentences. In fact, when it seemed more likely than not that his execution would be stayed, I drafted a final chapter called "Sixty," which was Carey's age throughout most of 2018. I thought that when I completed that chapter, he would have received yet another stay and have returned to what he called "living in limbo." In the final pages of that book, I would have explored how that made him feel. But that wasn't the ending that he and I were given.

The most vexing question I had to answer during the writing was, who was *I*? A friend who wanted to tell the life story of a man who inspired her so that others would be inspired by it, too? An activist who had seized an opportunity to address a social issue in order to effect change? An artist who took pleasure, as Annie Dillard said, in fashioning a text from the material at hand? Or an opportunist who was using a friend's afflictions as the subject of a book with her name on it? Perhaps I was all of these.

On the day of Carey's execution, I knew no peace until that evening, when I started writing the final chapter. Then, I knew with clarity and certainty who I was. I was the friend who wanted to commemorate a remarkable person and turn his suffering into good. I was the activist who wanted to end capital punishment in Nebraska, the United States, and the world. And I was the artist who found relief and comfort from a crushing sorrow by fashioning a text about it.

# Prologue

On the night of Tuesday, August 21, 1979, twenty-one-year-old Carey Dean Moore and his fourteen-year-old half-brother, Donald, went to a movie theater in downtown Omaha, Nebraska, then a city of 313,000 built into the bluffs and prairie west of the Missouri River. They ate at the Smoke Pit BBQ & Lounge on Twenty-Fifth and Farnam Streets. Then, they caught a taxi. The older Moore had planned for them to rob a cab driver that night. To prepare, they'd spent the past few days ordering cabs from a pay phone at the Greyhound bus depot and observing the drivers who showed up from afar.

The man they chose in the early hours of August 22 was forty-seven-year-old Reuel Van Ness Jr., who drove a Safeway cab. He arrived at the restaurant where the brothers were waiting to pick up his fare at 1:55 AM. Ten minutes later, the brothers climbed into his car. Moore directed Van Ness to drive them to Dam Site Sixteen at Standing Bear Lake, a new park northwest of Omaha. Because Van Ness didn't know the area, he called the dispatcher several times and asked a few fishermen for directions.

When Van Ness stopped his cab near a picnic area on the northside of the lake, the older Moore aimed his .32 automatic pistol at the back of his head and demanded that he hand over his money. Van Ness turned to grab the gun; Moore fired three shots, one each in Van Ness's head, hand, and near his spine. Burns on Van Ness's hand indicate that he had been reaching for the gun when Moore fired it. Donald dragged Van Ness's body from the cab, placed it on the ground, and then drove the cab back to Omaha while Carey mopped up the blood and wiped away their fingerprints.

The brothers parked about a half dozen blocks from their mother's downtown Omaha rowhouse apartment, split the money that they'd taken from Van Ness (seventy dollars according to most sources), then walked home. Police estimated that Van Ness may have died around 6:30 AM. Shortly thereafter, a man and woman who were fishing at the lake found his body in the middle of the road.

On Monday, August 27, Carey Moore returned to the cabstand at the Greyhound bus depot at Eighteenth and Farnam to select another, older cabbie. This time, he was alone. He was shocked to see that the first to respond to his call was indeed an older cabbie: his forty-nine-year-old mother, who drove a Happy Cab. Moore told her that he wanted a ride home, which she provided. Then he returned to the bus depot. This time Moore picked a forty-seven-year-old Happy Cab driver, Maynard D. Helgeland, and asked him to take him to the Benson neighborhood in North Omaha.

After arriving in Benson, Moore asked Helgeland to drive him back downtown. Near Twenty-Sixth Street and Dewey Avenue, Moore ordered the driver to stop the car and shot him in the head at close range. Helgeland appears not to have offered resistance. Moore pushed Helgeland's body out of the driver's seat and drove the cab to Twenty-Second and Leavenworth Streets. There, he wanted to search Helgeland's pockets for money, but because of all of the blood, he gave up and walked home empty-handed. Moore took Donald to the crime scene and showed him what he'd done. And at about six thirty Tuesday morning, a Greyhound bus driver saw Helgeland's body slumped in the cab and called the police, who placed Helgeland's time of death between nine thirty or ten o'clock Monday evening.

On June 20, 1980, Carey Dean Moore, who had confessed to his crimes, was sentenced to death for each of his two first-degree murder convictions. Donald F. Moore, then fifteen, was charged with first-degree murder on August 15, 1980; however, the charge was later changed to second-degree murder, which carried a ten-years-to-life sentence. Donald pled guilty and spent twenty-eight years in prison. After many years of refusing to appeal his sentence, Carey Dean Moore was executed by lethal injection on August 14, 2018, at the Nebraska State Penitentiary.

# I

# The Challenge

It was an execution that led to my twenty-three-year friendship with death row inmate Carey Dean Moore and another one that ended it.

On September 2, 1994, Harold Lamont "Wili" Otey was executed at the Nebraska State Penitentiary (NSP) in Lincoln for the 1977 rape and murder of Jane McManus. He was the first person that Nebraska had put to death in the electric chair since the 1959 execution of mass murderer Charles Starkweather. For a few years prior to Otey's execution, my children and I participated in vigils and protests against the fulfillment of this death sentence in particular and the death penalty in general. When we first started attending these gatherings, Meredith was a baby whom I carried in a baby carrier on my chest; and Ian was a rambunctious six-year-old who played with the children of other abolitionists. Some of us were members of Nebraskans Against the Death Penalty, some belonged to the NAACP, and some religious denominations were particularly well represented, including the Quaker meeting and the Unitarian Universalist, United Methodist, and Catholic churches. Only occasionally were there counter-protesters, though sometimes people yelled at us from their cars.

On the night of September 1, 1994, we were among the two thousand that gathered outside of the NSP, according to a *New York Times* estimate. Those of us opposing the execution were a solemn bunch: we sang, prayed, and held candles. But because Otey was a Black man and his victim a white woman, those clamoring for his death were even more vicious than the typical pro-execution crowd. People held signs with barbaric messages such as: "Nebraska State Pen First Annual BBQ"; "Buckwheat says Capital

Punishment is OTEY"; "Hey Willie [sic], it's Fryday"; and "Nebraska—the Good Life for Whites," the last two words being a qualification of our state slogan. Over the course of the evening, that crowd, a de facto lynch mob, moved from one chant to the next: "Barbecue!" and "Fry the nigger!" Some sported swastikas. Some crowd surfed. A hooded person carried a noose. A woman passing out French fries asked people if they wanted fries with their Otey. Students at the University of Nebraska–Lincoln brandished signs proclaiming their allegiance to a fraternity or sorority or a dormitory floor. That night, I looked into the heart of darkness.

I've opposed the death penalty for as long as I can remember. In part, my opposition is practical, as the death penalty is exorbitantly expensive and unfairly applied, doesn't deter crime, and occasionally results in the death of innocent people. But my chief opposition is grounded in my Christian faith. When Jesus came upon a group of Pharisees and teachers of the law who were about to stone a woman caught in the act of adultery, they set a trap for him. They reminded him that this was legal under Mosaic law. "Now what do you say?" they asked him. As usual, Jesus didn't deny the legality of a law but raised the bar for its implementation: only those without sin could cast the first stone at the woman. I understand this to mean that even though a society can have a death penalty on the books, Christians can't support it being carried out because no human has ever or will ever meet the qualification that Jesus set forth. And, too, the gospel message is that deep change can happen any time, any place, and to any person. By executing someone, we cut short that likelihood.

But what I saw on the night of Otey's execution is that the death penalty is about far more than exacting "life for life, eye for eye, tooth for tooth," a favorite Bible verse of its proponents. As Garrett Fagan writes in *The Lure of the Arena: Social Psychology and the Crowd at the Roman Games*, "the Romans were by no means alone in finding the sight of people and animals tormented and killed both intriguing and appealing." The zest and delight that I witnessed among many of the death penalty proponents on the night of Otey's execution was the same lust for death and mutilation expressed by the ancient Romans at the arena. That was an appetite that I didn't want either my elected officials or my tax dollars feeding.

Just days after Otey's execution, several dozen death penalty abolitionists and I gathered at a Lincoln church to mourn, console one another, and strategize. One woman, who had regularly visited Otey, challenged us to get to know people on death row so that those we were advocating for weren't abstractions but individuals, each with a family, a hometown, a unique life story, and hopes for the future. In November, I met that challenge by joining eight or so members of Nebraskans Against the Death Penalty (NADP) on one of their semiannual visits to death row.

And what a challenge it was. In the days leading up to the visit, I was nervous. I'm very claustrophobic, so just the thought of being inside a prison left me wondering if I could even go through with it. And if I did, what would it be like to meet men who'd killed one or more people? And what to wear that would be appropriate? Professional? Business casual? Smart casual? Something more relaxed? Bright or somber? I chose a plain top, a comfortable cardigan, blue slacks, and Birkenstock sandals. Nothing provocative, nothing that might make me stand out in a crowd.

Much about entering the prison unnerved me, from the check-in at the front desk, where I left my keys, belt, and purse in a locker (I feel naked without my purse), to the simple pat down (I had to relinquish the antacid in my pocket). Our next stop was what I'd come to call the "holding cage," a small room that was glassed and barred. After leaving the check-in and before being buzzed into the visitor's room, we were locked behind those bars for what was probably only a minute or two but seemed like twenty. "This is where you feel like wetting your pants," one of the other NADP-ers told me, the claustrophobic newbie, as the heavy door slid shut behind us.

In the visiting room, we waited for the inmates to arrive. I heard the other NADP-ers make small talk, but my thoughts were swirling and I was too busy looking around to fully join the conversation. In all of the crime shows I'd seen, Plexiglas separated the inmate and the visitor. I saw no such barrier here. General population inmates and their visitors sat in pairs, talking and eating junk food from the vending machines. The guard at the desk was armed. When the death row inmates arrived, I was nauseous and sweaty. Was this situation really safe? There were five of them, as half of those who were interested in visiting with NADP came to the first visit; the other half would come to the second visit on the next day. Four of the inmates were white, one was Native American, and all were in their thirties or forties. One wore civilian clothes; the others wore prison-issue tan pants, tan shirts, and white tennis shoes. Our visit was to last a couple of hours. How would I get through it? But when I saw the inmates and the NADP-ers hugging each other and how happy everyone was to see each other, I relaxed a bit.

We sat facing each other in two rows of immovable chairs. First, we conversed as a group, then in pairs or small groups, with each visitor moving from one seat to another so that we could talk to each inmate individually. This was as scary as entering the holding cage. What would I say to these men, each a convicted murderer, each living a life I couldn't imagine? Was my life as foreign to them as theirs was to me? Would they see me as just another do-gooder or as someone here out of curiosity, a tourist who'd return to her free and comfortable life when the visit ended?

The inmates seemed experienced at talking to a first-timer, and I felt more at ease as we conversed about current events, legal processes, prison life, their childhoods, their families, and mine. And they quickly divested me of my naïve notions that the men on death row were so defeated and depressed by their experiences that they were nothing but numbers in the prison-industrial complex awaiting their turn to die in the electric chair, people who had much to gain by knowing me but nothing to give me in return. But I could see that in so many ways, these were just regular men. They worked out, played sports, and followed the news, and most stayed in touch with their families through visits, phone calls, and letters. What marked them as different from me and my friends was their knowledge of the law, the court system, the appeals process, the failures of the criminal justice system, and their lack of free movement. They lived behind a series of locked doors, none of which they had a key for. I would learn of other ways in which their lives differed from mine, chiefly that they would forever be judged and identified by the worst act of their lives.

I had participated in the death row visit as a duty, but I'd laughed and learned so much that I vowed to return for NADP's spring visit. When it was time to leave, I, too, hugged the inmates.

During my first visit, Carey Dean Moore had not been at the Lincoln prison, as he was in Omaha for court proceedings regarding the legality of his death sentence. Fifteen years earlier, in 1979, he confessed that he had chosen his robbery and murder victims, Maynard Helgeland and Reuel Van Ness Jr., both forty-seven, because they were much older than him and so, he reasoned, easier to rob. In 1980, a three-judge panel chose a death rather than a life sentence because of the "exceptional depravity" aggravator set forth in the *Nebraska Revised Statutes*, which stated that first-degree murder was eligible for a death sentence if the killer's actions were "so coldly calculated as to indicate a state of mind totally and senselessly bereft of all regard for human life." In 1994, the Nebraska Supreme Court ruled that this aggravator was constitutionally vague "as written and constructed" and so vacated Carey's death sentence. Then, the court redefined the phrase in question, "exceptional depravity," as "cold, calculated planning of the victim's death as exemplified by the purposeful selection of a particular victim on the basis of special characteristics." As Carey chose Helgeland and Van Ness because of their age, his crimes now met the revised definition. On April 21, 1995, the state district court resentenced him to death. In May, when I visited death row for the second time, Carey Dean Moore was there.

I was immediately drawn to him. He had intelligent, light blue eyes and short, thinning blond hair, was soft-spoken though intense, and had a stutter that would come and go. ("Stop stuttering," he'd sternly tell himself, a command that he'd obey for awhile.) At thirty-seven, he was thirteen months younger than I. It was hard to believe that this man had ever done anything that met anyone's definition of "exceptional depravity." When he and I spoke individually, he asked the same questions as the other inmates had when we talked for the first time. Married? Yes. Kids? A daughter, Meredith, and a son, Ian. A job? I was an instructor at the University of Nebraska–Lincoln, where I'd recently received my PhD. But in August, I'd start a position as an assistant professor of English at Southern Illinois University in Carbondale. My son from an earlier relationship would move with me; my husband and I would share the long-distance parenting of our daughter, which meant that she'd move back and forth between her two homes a couple of times each month. What I didn't say was that we hoped that this arrangement would save our troubled marriage, a revelation that wasn't appropriate to share with someone I'd just met.

When the conversation turned to Carey, he didn't hold back. The first thing he told me about himself was unprompted: he had killed two people, he was guilty, and God had forgiven him. I had little experience talking with inmates and didn't know how rare such an admission was. Then he asked me something that none of the others had: "Are you a Christian?"

This is a question that makes me uneasy. People can have very different ideas about what it means to be a Christian. "I am," I answered warily.

"Praise God!" he exclaimed. "I am, too!"

We chatted about the church I belonged to. I told Carey that I grew up in the Methodist Church but that my family stopped attending when I was in my teens. The reason I'd joined Antelope Park Church of the Brethren in my early thirties was because I was drawn to the Brethren's pacifist "all war is sin" position as well as its commitment to social justice. I also liked the people there, and they had frequent—and fantastic—potlucks. He told me about reading his Bible from the first page of Genesis to the last page of Revelation, over and over, and that he couldn't survive in prison without God's help.

I told him that I prayed every morning: not the little flash prayers that I offered throughout the day, but during a time set aside for nothing but prayer. I had expected him, like most people, to be impressed. But he looked at me with wonder. "Is that all?" he asked. "Just once a day?" This was a man who spoke his mind; and apparently, he often paused for deep, sustained prayer. I was doubly impressed.

Toward the end of our time together, Carey asked me for my help. His pastor, who until recently had visited weekly, couldn't come anymore because of his advanced age and complications from his diabetes. Carey had written to many churches in Lincoln in hopes of finding someone who would engage with him in weekly Bible study and fellowship. Only a few clergymen answered; none was willing to visit him. When he asked if I would help him find a pastor, I said that I would ask my church about people who could see him regularly and promised to drop him a note about whatever I discovered. I couldn't have imagined then that my willingness to become involved with his search would lead to a friendship with a man who would be one of the greatest influences in my spiritual evolution.

I was pleased when George Eisele, a fellow member of my church, agreed to visit Carey twice a month. Our pastors, Dale and Christy Dowdy, said they would call on him as their schedule permitted. I wrote to Carey with the good news. A few days later, I opened my mailbox and removed an envelope addressed to my then-hyphenated last name. In the upper-left corner of the envelope was an address labeled with Carey's prison identification number, #32947, following his name. The letter was written front-to-back and with no margins on white, blue-lined paper in clear, penciled cursive. The envelope bore two stamps, enough postage to cover not only the cost of mailing the letter but of mailing the enclosed forms that George, Dale, Christy, and I would need to complete to be approved to visit Carey. Because I was moving to Illinois in August, I wouldn't be joining the team—at least at this time—and didn't fill out my form.

When I opened the letter and read the first few lines, Carey's exuberance and gratitude touched me.

> Dear Lisa: May 29th
>
> Hi! ☺ Monday, 8:03 am
>
> I've been waiting to hear from you. ☺ Glory unto God who reigns! Thank you so much for following through and for asking your pastors about some "weekly Christian fellowship" for me; I pray that our God will be thoroughly involved. ☺

We exchanged a few more warm but businesslike letters. Finally, nothing remained but the wait for George and the pastors' background checks to be completed and their visiting requests approved.

The challenge for me was what to do next. I'd met those on death row so that I would see them as real people instead of the names, crimes, and mugshots that I knew from the newspaper. I learned that the headlines didn't sum them up as human beings. I'd found the regular visitors that

Carey sought. Case closed, right? Certainly, I didn't have time for a pen pal or the desire to invest in a friendship that might end with my friend's execution. But then I received a four-page letter from Carey that had nothing to do with the visits. He again expressed his gratitude for my help in finding Christian friends for him followed by "PTL [Praise the Lord]!!!" and "Hallelujah!!!" and a smiley face. I'd never known anyone who said "PTL" with a straight face or used so many emojis and exclamation points. He asked what sports I liked (the only one he watched on TV was women's tennis); what I would be teaching at my new job in Illinois (creative nonfiction); how old my kids were (Ian, ten; Meredith, four); and what they liked (Ian: Boy Scouts, camping, art, *The Simpsons*; Meredith: violin, dancing, twirly dresses, and *Shining Train Station*). Carey spent almost an entire page asking questions similar to those that had filled our first conversation in the penitentiary visiting room. But then he suggested that we might move beyond small talk. "Oh, by the way," he added. "If you have 'anything' to ask me, go ahead, and I'll let you know if/when it becomes personal; and, if it's ok with you, I'll do the same" (June 10, 1995). This proposal was followed by two pages containing what he called "my little testimony," a skeletal history of his childhood, a story that he would flesh out with details, anecdotes, and discoveries over the next twenty-three years.

Carey was born in Omaha on October 26, 1957. Dave, his identical twin, arrived three minutes later. Carey already had five older sisters and a brother. Two more brothers were born after Dave, so the family consisted of these ten children and two half-siblings. Because their father didn't earn enough money at his factory and restaurant jobs to support such a large family, Carey's parents found adoptive homes for two of his younger brothers. "Clearly by this time, my dad was already spending most of his paycheck on booze (within time he became an alcoholic in the worst way) which was bad on the family," Carey wrote. "No food, lousy clothes, and we moved quite a lot since rent was hard to pay (thanks to dad)." When I was taking flute and dancing lessons and baking cakes for my Barbie dolls in my Easy-Bake Oven, some of Carey's siblings "encouraged & taught Dave & I to steal and break & entering in to stores and gas stations; we would bring the food home and anything else we could get. Then we began to steal bikes, and our criminal life began . . . We were abused by dad so much, all of us but esp. Dave, Rick & I (and between us three, Dave & I were mostly beat). Life was so violent at that time." Carey attributed his stutter to his fear of beatings. As I read this, I recalled how determined he had been to control it.

The letter went on to describe the things that Carey had tried to overcome, such as being separated from Dave. When the twins were ten or eleven, they were placed in foster homes in different towns by a judge who thought it wise to separate them. "After that we spent a lot of time trying to get back to each other," Carey reported. By the time he was seventeen, Carey had been in "6–7 foster homes, two training schools, several jails." That year, he and Dave were reunited at the Youth Development Center (YDC) in Kearney, what Carey called a "boy's training school." Later in a letter, he would describe the time following their reunion as "heaven on earth." When they were eighteen, they were discharged (Carey first, then Dave), and they met up in Omaha as planned.

"Well, I think this is it," he concluded that June 10 letter. "I left out some things I guess; if you'd like to ask any questions, be my guess [sic]. (If not, it's ok). And, if you would like to know about me and life . . . after Dave and I were discharged." In later letters, Carey would tell me about the three aimless years following his discharge from YDC, the birth of his daughter, "Mandy," whom he'd see but once, the murders, his arrest, and his life on death row since 1980.

He signed off on this letter in the same way, more or less, that he'd sign off on the more than 320 letters that he'd send me:

> Take care, Lisa, thank you again for all your help! ☺ Have a great week and drive safe. Write when you like to—(no obligation). ☺
> Your friend, Carey Dean
> P.S. Jesus loves you so much, Lisa! PTL!!!

How could I not write back?

# 2

# The Early Years

Carey and I spent the first several years of our correspondence introducing ourselves. He usually took the lead, writing frankly and sincerely. We quickly moved from small talk to self-disclosure, creating a friendship that survived those periods when I was either so absorbed by work and family that my responses were not as timely as I wish they'd been, or I could only schedule an occasional face-to-face visit, again because of my lack of availability. But we also experienced robust periods of exchange, especially when he was facing execution or in solitary confinement—or whenever I needed to turn to him for advice. Usually, I welcomed a letter from him, which almost always arrived a day or two after I sent mine; but sometimes reading them made me feel that I was a poor correspondent, both in the time it took me to respond to one of his missives and in my ability to match his vulnerability.

Our friendship took root and grew so quickly because in 1995, I had plenty to talk about with a willing listener who could offer wise advice. When I filed for divorce in May, about the same time that Carey and I met, I was still in love with my husband and thought that reconciliation might be possible. But as the summer progressed, I abandoned hope. Our divorce and child custody agreements were approved in Lancaster County court on July 20. Eleven days later, I moved to Carbondale, Illinois. Despite the divorce and relocation, I was optimistic that my life would soon be less fraught and more fulfilling. That August, I began an exciting but demanding position as an assistant professor of English at Southern Illinois University, my first experience teaching graduate students. That fall, my dissertation,

*Field of Vision*, a collection of autobiographical nature essays, was accepted for publication at the University of Iowa Press and would be published the following year. Professionally, I was thriving.

But I quickly discovered that living with the consequences of the divorce was sad and frustrating. Because of my discomfort with asserting myself and my inexperience with negotiating under difficult circumstances, I had given away too much. Our joint custody arrangement required that Meredith, who was four and a half at the time, fly back and forth between her two homes twice a month. For me, that meant a 140-minute drive between my home in Carbondale and the St. Louis airport, and an equally long return home. Meredith spent about 55 percent of her time with her father and 45 percent with me, as my ex-husband argued that she needed to remain at the excellent Montessori school that she had been attending since her third birthday. The two and a half years in which my little daughter and I were apart more than we were together were one of the most painful trials I've ever endured.

Because Ian was from an earlier relationship of mine, he wasn't included in the joint-parenting agreement with my ex-husband. We celebrated his eleventh birthday in our new home, and a few days later, he entered fifth grade at a new school. I found a small, friendly church for my children and me, and we got acquainted with our neighbors. It was easier to make fast friends—fast as in forming quickly, fast as in resistant and durable—in Carbondale than in any other place I've lived. I was grateful for the ease with which my children and I filled our lives with good people. But I wasn't at peace: I was far from home, felt overwhelmed by the workload, and missed my daughter fiercely when she wasn't with me. Now I wonder if my friendship with Carey would have developed as quickly or as deeply if we had met during a more stable time in my life. Even though I was working through these challenges with a therapist, Carey also helped me to process them, and I enjoyed his self-revelations and his warm, personal voice. For me, becoming his friend was one of the most significant events of 1995.

That was an eventful year for him, too. In 1994, the Eighth Circuit Court of Appeals had vacated his death sentence over questions regarding the meaning of the "exceptional depravity" aggravator. I wondered what it was like for him to live with the possibility of being placed in the general prison population with two life sentences. Had a terrible heaviness lifted? But then, another had taken its place. On April 21, 1995, a three-judge panel of the state district court resentenced him to death on two counts of felony murder after redefining the term in question.

That year, Carey also lost his pastor but gained new friends at Antelope Park Church of the Brethren in Lincoln. Perhaps he counted this growing alliance with George Eisele, Pastors Dale and Christy, and me—achieved through letters, telephone calls, and visits—as another major event. As our friendship grew, Carey and I began to provide enough backstory to piece together the early periods of each other's lives as we shared current and ongoing events. I suspect that Carey either wanted new correspondents to know the story of his childhood or felt that it was something they expected; and so, he provided it without being asked. This particular story had a more rehearsed or well-revised feel, as opposed to his typically relaxed and spontaneous voice.

Across many letters written during the first several years of our friendship and in the summer of 2018, Carey elaborated on the initial, skeletal story that he'd told me in a letter from June 10, 1995, speaking in more detail about the effect that poverty and his father's alcoholism had on the family and his relationship with his twin brother, Dave. Though he said that all of the Moore children suffered physical abuse, he and Dave suffered the most. Three of Carey's siblings told the three-judge panel that sentenced their brother to death in 1980 that their father had beaten him with "electrical cords and leather straps." Apparently, there was no intervention, since, as Carey wrote, he "was badly abused by dad at a time where cops and most judges thought that a dad ought to punish and discipline his own children" (December 5, 2002). But surely no authority would approve of a man who caused his son to live in such fear of beatings that he stuttered.

Carey was probably too young to realize what was happening when his parents found adoptive parents for their two youngest sons, reasoning that separation from the family wouldn't be as damaging to them as it would have been for the older children. Mr. and Mrs. Moore gave one son, who was a year younger than Carey, to a family across the street and the youngest child, Bartley Joseph, to a family from Colorado. But even with fewer children to provide for, the family's circumstances remained bleak. "Thanks to my dad, we were still very poor, hungry, and I do not remember about how our clothes looked though we went to the Salvation Army stores a lot" (December 2, 2002). I wonder if in time, he feared—or hoped—that his parents might give him away, too.

Carey said little about school. Perhaps that was because his education was so disrupted that he didn't have memories of science fairs, sports teams, school plays, and the like. Perhaps it was because his stutter and Salvation Army clothes made him the target of other children. He and Dave were in "a Omaha 'Youth Center' for juveniles [. . .] many times from maybe 7 to 9 years old, just in & out for a couple months at a time" (July 17, 2018). In a letter written on July 3, 2018, Carey summarized what he'd told me about his childhood in bits and pieces over the years: "Dave, I, and our two-year older brother Rick had sort of an unusual childhood. Our fun was breaking into stores/gas stations/houses/buildings/schools and stealing things, skipping school, shop lifting, we did so much; we ran wild late at night, we were out of control [. . .] although we were never abusive or physical toward our mom or sisters." Toward the end of her marriage, Carey's mother, who "was lonely I guess," had an affair and became pregnant. Carey said that his father probably knew that Donald wasn't his biological child, and he and his wife "argued a lot about it of course" (July 9, 2018). When Carey was nine, his parents separated and divorced after twenty years of marriage. Carey wrote that his father was ordered to pay his mother forty dollars per week in child support for nine children. (In 2022, that's the equivalent of about $347 per week or about $1,388 per month.) During the divorce, his father "gave us permission to do as we pleased; we were already doing that! Dad was always drinking and in his drunken-mind he wanted to show the judge that he was 'needed' in the home and therefore their divorce shouldn't be granted; we told mom, she told the judge, the judge was mad" (July 3, 2018).

When the twins were "9 or 10 or 11 years old" and "royal brats," they were sent to different foster homes, and Carey lived for awhile at Cristo Rey, a Catholic group home in Lincoln. "The judge who separated us felt it was to our best interest if we were divided, even hundreds of miles [. . .] throughout this state because I kept doing things to get out of foster homes & training school, just to try to get back to Dave; he was in only 2–3 foster homes which one home was very abusive toward him—and they went to church!" (July 9, 2018). The separation from his twin was so painful that Carey likened it to "hard labor."

After his parents separated, Mrs. Moore, who had been a stay-at-home mother, became a Tupperware dealer and started keeping company with a man whom she'd eventually marry. Carey and his future stepfather had a contentious relationship:

> We almost never got along with each other when he began dating my mom, I was maybe 12 years old; he kicked my butt royally shortly after they met, because I slammed a door on Donny's (brother) fingers, who was maybe 5–6 at the time. This incident with him [the stepfather] caused my disrespect for him to grow. After this incident of being beat up by him, I began to steal his money whenever he came over to spend the weekend with my mom while they slept together in the morning hours; we're talking about several times and several hundred dollars (serious) (July 5, 1995).

When Carey was twelve or thirteen and "in training school" at Geneva, 125 miles southwest of Omaha, his mother remarried (July 5, 1995). She and her new husband had a daughter in 1969. Though Carey didn't like his stepfather, he said that he and his siblings accepted their new stepsister. (September 9, 1996). Whenever Carey "came 'home'" to his mother and stepfather's house, he "felt like a stranger" and thought that he shouldn't be there. "So, naturely [sic] perhaps, I got into trouble with the law and was therefore sent away to training schools, boy's homes, foster homes, and where I also felt more like a stranger (and possibly like an outsider and enemy). It seemed like an endless circle at times."

Carey spoke in general terms of the abuse he suffered while in foster care, but only offered one anecdote. When he was fourteen or fifteen, he was placed with foster parents in Mitchell, South Dakota. When his foster father "tried to do something homosexual with me" on a camping trip, Carey "wouldn't have nothing to do with it." He knew that he had to get away. When he and his foster father returned home, Carey stole and forged a check, then used it to buy a Greyhound bus ticket. "Maybe 50–70 miles away, the cops stopped me, threw me in jail and I told my story. They gave me a polygraph test which I past [sic], the foster dad tried to get me back but the cops or county attorney refused and sent me back to Omaha; I went into another foster home, no therapy if I needed it. I was in jail for a couple weeks there in S.D." (July 3, 2018). This story raised questions for me. Had Carey's foster parents been adequately screened and monitored? Had the authorities placed a fifteen-year-old boy in what I'm guessing was an adult correctional facility?

When Carey was around sixteen, he was sent to what was originally called the Nebraska State Reform School, which had opened in Kearney in 1881 to house "wayward children." A decade after its founding, it was renamed the State Industrial School for Juvenile Offenders and was tasked with preparing boys to earn a livelihood after release. When Carey was sent there, it was called the Youth Development Center or YDC, but he always referred to it as the "boys' training school." While there, he "surrendered my heart to Jesus and then was baptized by a Lutheran minister" (July 5, 1995). Carey never explained if this was the result of divine intervention, a persuasive pastor, peer pressure, or the desire to position himself in a group that received approval from those in charge. I suspect that it was more the first two reasons than the last two. When he was seventeen, his most fervent dream came true. "I was already at YDC, when one of the boys told me that he saw someone who looked just like me and I knew it had to be Dave—and it was; in spite of being at a training school, we were happy, finally together! Heaven on earth!" (July 19, 2018). After all those years of separation, all the punishment they'd endured for having run away from their respective situations to find each other, the twins were reunited. Once I asked Carey if he had a fond memory of childhood, as all the stories he'd told me about this time in his life were marked by pain, frustration, or sadness. "Teaching Dave how to swim in the YDC pool," he said.

Though Carey had become a Christian and had been baptized, he still got in trouble. On one occasion, his father and Dave's girlfriend made the 190-mile drive from Omaha to Kearney to visit the twins and take them out to eat. After the meal, the boys told their father that they were going to steal a car and flee, which they did. It's curious that they announced these intentions. Had they wanted their father to help them escape? Or to stop them? Mr. Moore reported their escape to YDC officials, but it was two weeks before the boys were returned to Kearney (July 14, 2018). Where had they gone? How had they met their needs for food, gas, and a place to sleep? How and where were they captured? What were the repercussions of this escape? At the time that I heard this story, I didn't ask for more details, perhaps because we were out of time, perhaps because it didn't occur to me. Once Carey started running away, he developed an appetite for it and couldn't stop.

In several of the stories that Carey told me about his childhood, he seemed to be saying that if his mother had been tougher with him or if he'd received harsher punishment while in custody, that his life might have turned out differently. For instance, when he was caught stealing cigarettes and sentenced to a few weeks in jail, either his mother or a close friend paid the fifty-dollar fine. "But, that was a bad mistake for the person to do that since I did NOT learn my lessons (as perhaps I might had, even though I appreciated being fined out of jail [. . .]. While in jail for the cigarettes, I felt so ashamed (for being there for stealing cigarettes)" (May 27, 2002).

When he first wrote to me about his time at YDC, my teenage son was struggling with so much, both in and out of school. Carey drew from his experiences—at YDC and in prison—to advise my son and me in the letters that he wrote to us. Carey always advocated for leaving a child to face the consequences of his or her actions, no matter how slight or destructive those consequences might be. Often, he was critical of me for making life "too easy" for my son and said that I was sending the wrong message to a "troubled kid" (September 19, 2002). I understood his arguments for tough love but doubted that it worked as well as Carey claimed and wondered how he might have turned out if the adults in his life had shown him more concern and provided more guidance and encouragement. While Carey and I discussed our differences on this matter, neither of us changed our position.

When he turned eighteen, Carey was discharged from YDC several weeks before Dave and stayed with his brother's girlfriend. While they were waiting for Dave to join them in Omaha, she introduced Carey to her friend "Dawn," "a pretty blond she was with brown eyes," he wrote in a 1995 poem. A month after they'd started seeing each other, Dawn said that she wanted to stop taking birth control pills. Carey agreed to this, yet was "floored" when she told him that she was pregnant a month or so later. In response, he stole a car. "Driving away I felt such an exaggerated sense of freedom, / though I knew it wasn't real. / I came to my senses . . . had to stick by my girl." But before he could do that, he was arrested for auto theft and spent thirteen months in jail. "Was I ever stupid," he wrote. In a telephone conversation after his arrest, Dawn told him goodbye, which left Carey feeling "dead and six feet under." While he was in jail, he received a letter from her that claimed she *wasn't* pregnant, but he didn't believe her. After his release, he searched for her and eventually found her living with a man. Just as Dawn was telling him that she didn't want to see him, a baby entered the room in a walker. Carey immediately recognized the child as his. I don't know if he attempted to maintain contact with his daughter at that time. While he was on death row, Dawn sent him a picture of their eleven-year-old daughter, "Mandy," through one of Carey's sisters. She was "so pretty," he wrote. He concluded in his poem that he was "hoping/ and praying that God will somehow bring us together—/ for a new beginning for my child and me."

In 1998, Carey's attorney and friend, Alan Peterson, hired a detective to search for Mandy. The detective discovered details about who, where, and when Dawn married and that Mandy was born on October 29, 1976, three days after Carey's nineteenth birthday. "Even though I am 'still' praying & hoping that before I die, my daughter Mandy and I will meet—and even get to know each other as best as possible under the circumstances; even though I am still praying, I had felt a little hopeless, like perhaps we wouldn't meet. 'Except in heaven'" (December 2, 2000). Sadly, his intuition was correct. In 2018, I offered to search for Mandy on social media, but Carey asked me not to. I often thought that reading or hearing about events that I shared with my children but that he couldn't share with his daughter—science fairs, parent-teacher conferences, recitals, church camp, holiday celebrations, homework, chores, allowances, and family road trips—caused him pain, especially when I considered that he hadn't received such attention himself as a child. But he was always interested, praising Ian's and Meredith's successes and giving advice or commiserating over their struggles.

When Carey was eighteen or nineteen, one of the two boys who Mr. and Mrs. Moore had given up for adoption was reintroduced into the family

(December 21, 2000). Around that time, Carey also saw his father for the first time in many years:

> When I remembered who he was, I remembered how mean & cruel he had been with his entire family before my mom divorced him in 1969. When I seen him as a young man of 18, he was living in a cheap smelly, run down hotel (in downtown Omaha); he looked so old beyond his age (around 50) from drinking during so many years & seeming still an alcoholic. He looked so sad & drained of life . . . It was an ugly sight, Lisa. This "man" was my dad (February 28, 1998).

Carey offered this story because I'd written to him about a meeting between my son and his biological father. During the first six years of his life, my son saw "Gerald" about a half dozen times. After I married in 1990, Gerald stopped calling and visiting. But in January 1998, when Ian was thirteen, I arranged for the two to meet in Kansas City. It had been so long since Ian had seen his biological father that he couldn't remember what he looked like. In the months that followed, Gerald attempted to establish a relationship with Ian but often canceled, didn't show up for visits, or didn't make the phone calls he'd scheduled. He also failed to send the money that he'd promised. Yet Ian never abandoned hope that someday the two of them would have a *real* father-son relationship.

I shared all of this with Carey, who offered his blunt assessment of the situation:

> I'm curious when Ian will wonder what you could possibly see in his dad, and when he'll ask you (if he hasn't done so already), or perhaps he may think to himself that maybe he should take another (long?) look at his dad to try to find what you must had seen in him [. . .]. And, if this is true, then if he will possibly respect or admire you for this "brief" time in your life. What do you think? The reason I think of this is because I might think that way myself, if I were in his shoes I mean. "Gerald" sounds like dirt, Lisa ☺ (February 28, 1998).

Carey's assessment of Gerald was correct and honest. But his words stung. And, too, they made me realize that I hadn't yet considered what the story of Ian's father and my relationship with him might mean to my son years hence. Indeed, I struggled to know what to say to Ian about his father's treatment of him at that moment. What I would eventually tell Ian, without going into detail, was that though I had seen the early warning signs about Gerald's character, I had stayed with him too long. What was easy to tell him was that though I didn't want Gerald, I was so very grateful to have my son. When Ian was twenty-four, Gerald, burdened by crushing debt, a failed business deal, and the death of his beloved dog, hanged himself from a tree in his backyard. It had been seven years since he and Ian had seen each other. Despite all of the hurt and disappointments that Ian had received from this man, he was willing, as Gerald's next of kin, to help clean up Gerald's house, finances, and legal matters. When I told Carey the news of Gerald's suicide, he was uncharacteristically reserved. But he sent his condolences and assured me that Ian was in his prayers (March 20, 2009).

When Carey asked about my childhood, I told him that I had grown up in Burlington, a small city in southeast Iowa on the Mississippi River. My mother was a biology teacher; my father was a boilermaker at the CB&Q—later Burlington Northern—Railroad. There was much that was right about my childhood: my parents had stable, respectable jobs, and we had all the good food we wanted. My grandparents and a doting great aunt lived nearby. Plus, there was money for extras like a flute, a piano, and private lessons for me; orthodontics and musical instruments for my two brothers; allergy shots for one of my brothers and me. I didn't wear thrift store clothing until I was an adult, and then by choice. My parents expected us to go to college, and we did, though none of us did the traditional four years right out of high school. Each of us entered a profession (professor, engineer, pilot) that provided a good living and meaningful work. When I compared my life to Carey's, I felt uneasy and apologetic about all the privileges that I'd benefited from, privileges that he lacked through no fault of his own. And yet, mine wasn't a perfect childhood. My parents drank too much; still, neither missed work because of it. My father was dutiful, though at times, emotionally absent. My vivacious, impulsive, and nurturing mother had extramarital affairs, which she began confiding to me when I was in high school. When I was in my twenties, I suspected that my youngest brother was actually my half-brother, but I kept my suspicions to myself until my grandmother confirmed them in 1997. This was a secret I carried until 2016, when my brother received puzzling results from a DNA test, and a difficult revelation for him and my other brother. But when I considered Carey's childhood, I felt I had no right to complain about anything.

I was blessed to have my father until 2006 and my mother until 2016. On May 1, 1984, toward the end of Carey's third year in prison, his father died of a heart attack. Several months would pass before the Moore children learned of this. His mother had beaten cancer once, but it returned with a vengeance. On June 13, 1984, she died at the age of fifty-four. Carey loved his mother, who "had her share of heartache and grief" (November 23, 2001), and regretted that she'd had such a hard life. Carey wrote that at times, her punishments were harsh "but then again we drove her NUTS much of the time; actually, she was very patient as much as possible but our antics and trouble making ways drove her crazy some" (May 4, 2018). In her last letter to Carey, which he quoted to me on several occasions, she wrote: "'Remember, God loves you even more than I do.' I know she loved me so much, so naturally, He must love me A LOT! ☺" (July 23, 2018).

Still, as the adult children of alcoholics, Carey and I had profound similarities. Two common traits of such people are their avoidance of conflict at any cost and internalizing rather than expressing their feelings. "For years, Lisa, I kept feelings and thoughts almost bottled up, which I suppose also jumbled up everything, and which also had a big influence on me when I came to murder two men" (July 5, 1995). In the last month of his life, Carey told me about how overwhelming his anger could be once he expressed it:

> There's an old saying or something like that that says—"Step on a crack you break your momma's back" . . . well, when I was possibly 11–12–13, I was in a boys & girls training school in Geneva, NE. Oh, she [his mother] meant to visit me during a Saturday or Sunday but couldn't come, but all week long I wanted to see her but she didn't show up and all day I was so mad and every time I was outside I'd step on a crack on the sidewalk and say, "Step on a crack break your momma's back." That gave me relief but of course years later I took it all back! No doubt. Yes, when I was younger, I was full of anger and rage, which someplaces [sic] I was at, well, it was simply too bad for all of us. Usually I was nice but sometimes, Lisa, it had to spill out (July 14, 2018).

Because of Carey's choice of the word "rage" and the lack of an illustrating example, I had to wonder just how bad that anger could be.

When I was a child, I, too, tried to keep things peaceful. But it was a superficial peace, achieved by tamping down my feelings and by not mentioning anything, great or small, that might make my parents uncomfortable and cause explosions, meltdowns, or withdrawals. This was a pattern of behavior that hasn't served me well—then or now. Like Carey, I wait too long to say what is bothering me. He commiserated:

> I'm glad you shared about "how you tried to keep things peaceful as a child"; very interesting, Lisa. I do know what you mean. I also tried (and sometimes had no success whatsoever, and had at times made it worse) to keep the peace in many stressful situations; and many, many times I hated this side of me. [. . .] You wrote: "We had a big split in my family about 4 years ago. It is somewhat healed, but the spooky thing is, no one dare talk about the problem, then or now. [. . .] When I write to my 4 of

my 6 sisters [...] it is so difficult to get answers to personal questions (past and present), like extracting a tooth from a gorilla who's not asleep or doped up! ☺ (July 18, 1995).

Because of these early influences and patterns that taught my friend to ignore problems and to stifle his emotions, I found it remarkable and admirable that the Carey I knew was so open, honest, and direct.

In November of 2000, the Moore family received surprising news. That year, Bartley Joseph, whose adoptive parents had named John, applied for a passport and traveled from his home in Colorado to Omaha to get the required birth certificate. John knew he was adopted, but when he saw the names of his biological parents, Norman and Eleanor Moore, he decided to try to find them. "The same day he got his b.c., he looked in the telephone book for 'Moore' and prayed to God to help him dial the right number (I was overjoyed when he said he'd pray to find us!) and on his second attempt, he was speaking to [one of Carey's sisters] ☺ " That Thanksgiving, another sister hosted a dinner at her home in John's honor and "about 30 of his 'new' relatives showed up" (December 21, 2000). On November 29, John was granted a one-hour visit with Carey at the Nebraska State Penitentiary (NSP). "We talked & talked & talked & talked! [...] Just consider a couple weeks ago, not any of this had happened—God can change everything. God has changed EVERYTHING!" (December 2, 2000). Even though the detective that Alan Peterson had hired to locate Carey's daughter hadn't been able to find the information that might have brought the two together, John's discovery of his birth family gave Carey new hope of finding his daughter.

John and his wife, Glory, whom I became acquainted with over lunch in 2003 when they came to Lincoln to visit Carey, developed a close, nurturing relationship with him. Because they lived in Colorado and later New York, when John and Glory visited they got permission from prison authorities to do so for several days in a row. John delivered sermons at the funerals of two of the Moore sisters. Together, he and Glory offered a moving eulogy at Carey's memorial service.

The most poignant family stories that Carey told were about the devotion that he and Dave—Carey's great and loyal supporter in terms of visits, emotional support, and money—felt toward each other. As twins, they had parallel experiences, not just in utero but through the abuse, the wild adventures, the juvenile delinquency, the long, painful separations that resulted from being state wards in foster homes, the reformatories and prisons, and joyous reunions.

In one of his first letters to me, Carey included an excerpt from a letter that Dave had written to him about the nature of their relationship:

My brother, Dave, wrote me a letter last week and it was extremely emotional! Praise God! I've been praying for Dave for so long, and yes, we talk about Jesus though I try not to hit him over the head with it every opportunity I'd get. Anyway, his letter was about the Death Penalty and if I am executed either by the State or if I gave up my appeals. Dave writes, "I love you, with a love no word can describe, Dean [Carey's family calls him that]. I will miss you, just as I would miss a part of my body. But I do understand. My heart becomes heavy, just to imagine you not being here. I will keep your ashes nearby for when I need to talk to you or when the missing becomes unbearable. I, too, will then wish for death, where we might be together as in one. I will keep searching until I find you, and with God's grace, be permitted to remain as one" (July 31, 1995).

Both men were in NSP at the same time—Carey for murder and Dave for theft. A story that Carey didn't mention in his letters but told me about in person, one that I would read about in the *New York Times* decades after it happened, concerns the twins changing places in NSP. During a contact visit in October 1984 to discuss family business (likely related to the death of one or both of their parents), the two traded clothes and positions, so that Dave was sitting in Carey's death row cell and Carey was in the prison kitchen where Dave worked. It was the kitchen supervisor who realized that something was up since "Dave" was suddenly ten to fifteen pounds heavier and had a ruddier complexion. And, too, "Dave" asked another inmate where to put a pan that he'd just dried, something the real Dave would have known.

Some considered this a prank, others an escape attempt. Either way, Carey and Dave lost contact visits for over fifteen years, which grieved them. They could only speak through telephones and with glass between them. On Christmas Day 1995, Carey wrote to Warden Hopkins that he'd be willing to have one foot shackled during contact visits if that meant being in the same room as Dave. "I would also like to add that Dave has two tatoos [sic], one on his arm and one on his back; I do not have any tatoos. Do you have any suggestions, Mr. Hopkins." The next day, Carey received the warden's written denial of his request. "I am not comfortable with your suggestions and don't have any to offer at this time."

When the warden finally allowed the twins a contact visit at 5:00 PM on December 11, 1999, Carey wrote, "It was strange for both of us to be with each other 'face to face,' without having a glass window in front of us & speaking on phones. This was a one-hour and a one-time visit although I will ask again for another visit perhaps in June, I think" (January 13, 1999).

During Carey's first month at Tecumseh State Correctional Institution (TSCI), Nebraska's new medium- and maximum-security prison, "the front entrance goofed up & allowed us 'Contact' visits, but then of course they caught it and now once again we have No Contact Visits; what a bummer" (July 26, 2002). After a long campaign that involved numerous "kites," written requests to prison staff and letters to various officials, including state senator Ernie Chambers, regular contact visits were restored to the brothers about twenty years ago, though Carey continued to be shackled during visits until 2016 (July 9, 2018).

Carey cherished his Sunday morning visits with Dave. Sometimes, Dave brought his then-wife and daughter, but after he and his wife divorced, he usually came alone. It was harder for Dave to visit Carey at TSCI in Tecumseh than at NSP in Lincoln because he was already commuting between Lincoln and Crete, a small town about twenty-five miles southwest of Lincoln, for his night shift at Farmland Foods Inc. If Dave's work schedule changed, Carey told George and me not to come on Wednesday, the only other day for visits with death row inmates, because Dave would be there.

On more than one occasion, Carey said that the only person who could keep him from "volunteering," or not fighting his execution, was Dave. "I was thinking a couple days ago (again) that if it weren't for Dave I probably wouldn't be here today—(I'm pretty sure)" (October 16, 1998). And yet, Carey knew that Dave wouldn't ask him to fight execution. "It sounds strange to say this sort of, but I don't think Dave would ask me 'not' to stop my appeals because he knows & understands how I feel, and if he was in my shoes, he wouldn't want me to ask him 'not' to . . . I don't know what I would say to Dave if he did ask me not to. But, I'm sure I know my brother very well. Praise God!" (April 22, 1998). However, if Mandy showed up and said she wanted to get to know him, he would fight his execution, "since it's the very least I could do for her" (April 22, 1998).

During the first several years of our growing friendship, Carey and I wrote often about the big events in our lives. But our letters were also filled with the everyday and commonplace, the little things that friends chat about over coffee in each other's homes or on a walk in the park: what we were reading; what was in the news (the O. J. Simpson trial; Clinton's impeachment; Karla Faye Tucker, whose charismatic personality and conversion to Christianity caused many to oppose her 1998 execution; 9/11; the case of Michael Bruce Ross, who stopped his appeals and volunteered for his 2005 execution in Connecticut); television programs (*Sex and the City*; *The Lawrence Welk Show*; *Touched by an Angel*); people that we both knew; the birth of Dave's daughter, Taylor Kari; teaching my kids to drive; Carey's knee injury, his jogging, his poetry; Ian's first job; Meredith's appendectomy;

my parents' move to Ohio; encounters with difficult people; money, prayer, and what was for lunch. I wrote to Carey about the homemade pizzas Meredith and I made. My favorite toppings were sauerkraut, black olives, and extra tomatoes. Meredith ate this, but Ian wasn't a fan of the sauerkraut; he wanted red meat and hot peppers. Carey responded, "It was 'funny' that Ian put 'hot sauce' on the pizza which is how I like it, and yes—I did tell him! ☺ My hot sauce is Picante sauce (extra hot) plus I also add jalapeno peppers to it so it's even hotter. I perspire pretty good after I'm finished eating! ☺ I'm glad you liked your pizza!" (October 1, 1998).

Because Carey lived in a prison, there were physical barriers that were hard or impossible to cross. We could visit in person, but only at the prison and only at set times. We could talk by telephone, but only if he called me, only at certain times, and only if I paid for the calls. We couldn't engage in typical activities like taking a Saturday road trip, meeting for a meal in a restaurant or each other's homes, or showing up at the hospital or funeral home when the other's family member was ill or deceased. Consequently, our friendship was carried on primarily through the written word. This was a friendship that could go deep; and yet, there were limits on it, which made it easier to avoid the messiness of some male-female friendships that I'd experienced.

Equally formidable were the challenges that arose because Carey and I lived on different sides of several socially constructed boundaries created by income, education, religion, and politics (he was a Republican; I usually vote Democrat). But by listening to and responding to each other's stories with open hearts, we found ways over, under, or around those walls.

On February 28, 1998, Carey wrote: "By the way, Lisa, I'm glad to hear from you! ☺ ☺ ☺ Really, I count you as one of my close friends, praise God!!!"

The feeling was mutual.

# 3

# The Rest of the Story

At our first meeting, Carey told me that he'd killed two men. Both in his letters and in person, he frequently expressed remorse for the murders and their effects on his family, the families of his victims, and himself. But he rarely spoke about his life at the time and gave even fewer details about the killings themselves. When *Lincoln Journal Star* reporter Cory Matteson asked Carey to tell the story of the murders days after his seventh stay of execution in 2011, Carey said that he was willing to answer any question but that one.

I never asked about that pivotal week in my friend's life, nor did I have any desire to read the trial transcripts. For the most part, it was enough for me to know that he had changed profoundly from the man who'd brutally ended two lives all those years ago. But there seemed to be more than that. Perhaps I wanted to avoid the discomfort of having to hold two irreconcilable aspects of the same person in my mind, fearing that if I learned more about how my friend had killed Van Ness and Helgeland beyond what I'd read in the newspaper, I would feel differently about him. And, too, I worried that my questions would distress him. But finally, just months before his execution, I asked, and only because I had to have his version of the murders for this book.

"Gosh, Lisa, writing or even speaking about days and weeks prior to the murders has always been so very difficult for me," Carey wrote when I posed the question (June 20, 2018). But over the course of several letters, he answered my questions anyway. "It's like digging through the cobwebs I guess. If you have questions on that, just ask; if I forgot, than [*sic*] I forgot"

(July 3, 2018). I was impressed that he was willing to speak openly about something he found so painful—especially when he knew that his words would end up in print. I hoped that as he awaited his execution, he found it comforting to know that the story that mattered most to him, the one about the deep, all-encompassing change that he'd experienced being made possible through God's love and power, would be available to those who needed it.

In August 1979, Carey was living in Omaha with his mother, who rented an apartment in downtown Omaha after leaving her second husband. She worked as a Happy Cab driver and Tupperware dealer (July 14, 2018). Fourteen-year-old Donald, the youngest child in the family and Carey's half-brother, whom the *Omaha World-Herald* described as a "high school drop-out," also lived with them. Carey's circumstances were grim: with a tenth-grade education, he could only get restaurant or factory jobs, none of which he kept for very long. As he had no driver's license, he rode the bus; in order to take out a woman that he wanted to impress, he stole a car. He had nearly hit rock bottom:

> Maybe for a month or two before the murders, my self-esteem was so low, and one time during that time mom saw something and suggested to me that I should see a shrink or therapist but of course I rejected that suggestion, besides it was another bill and I didn't or couldn't trust anyone. I couldn't even tell mom what was going on inside of me, or maybe I couldn't even understand myself (June 20, 2018).

A news clip from shortly after the murders shows Carey in a white T-shirt, with a light mustache, a darker jaw beard, and, already, a receding hairline. His eyes are downcast as the officer holding Carey's muscled upper arm escorts him through what appears to be a courthouse. In a newspaper photograph from that time, Carey's face is lean and clean-shaven; his blond hair is wavy and shoulder length. His eyes are light, intense, and upward-looking. The impertinent expression on his face is one that I'd never seen on him.

A week or so before the murders, Carey and Donald were "searching through cars" when they found several checks. Carey forged the signature and gave them to a trusted friend, who cashed the checks at his workplace. With the money—about $1,100, according to the *Omaha World-Herald*—Carey bought marijuana, alcohol, and white crosses, an amphetamine. About the same time, the man with whom Carey's mother shared Happy Cab number 64, offered to sell her son a .32 automatic pistol. Carey's mother ordered him not to buy it—"She probably knew what would happen if I got my hands on a gun," Carey wrote (June 20, 2018)—but he took one hundred dollars of what remained from the forged checks and bought the gun anyway.

At the time, Carey believed his life was utterly hopeless. "While I was thinking about his offer [to buy the gun] during the last week while on drugs, I thought of the Death Penalty if I got caught in a robbery and killed the man but I decided that it didn't matter, wouldn't matter" (June 20, 2018). Perhaps he couldn't imagine a future that might be different. Perhaps he was so miserable that he felt that his life had already ended.

While Carey and I were sitting in the visiting room at NSP (which means that the visit occurred before 2002, as death row was moved to the new prison in Tecumseh that year), he told me a story that puzzled me; in fact, I found it so bizarre that I didn't understand what he was trying to tell me. When Carey related the story again in a letter written on July 3, 2018, he connected his actions to the murders both in time and in significance. When Carey is addressing difficult subject matter, he tends to write run-on sentences, as in the following passage:

> Here's something completely embarrassing & humiliating: just a week or two before the cab murders, I was walking up a hill (in front of Nebraska Furniture Mart downtown) and an elderly woman was walking down, as I passed by her, I reached out and grabbed her breast when she screamed out, I laughed being surprised at myself. My point is, I had to sink to a low level.

Carey believed that at the moment when he grabbed the woman's breast, he had crossed a line in his thinking and actions that made it possible for him to commit murder. When I encountered this story a second time, I was distressed both by what he'd done to the woman and by the thought that if someone could have intervened just before the arrival of that pivotal moment, his life might have taken a different turn. So, too, might have the lives of Reuel Van Ness Jr., Maynard Helgeland, and their families.

But there was no intervention. And so, one August evening in 1979, Carey and Donald found themselves at the Smoke Pit BBQ & Lounge eating sandwiches while waiting for their taxi to arrive. At 1:55 AM, Reuel Van Ness Jr. entered the restaurant and called out that "Bill's" cab had arrived. Van Ness was a forty-seven-year-old Korean War veteran, husband, and father of ten children—six from his wife, Louise's, earlier marriage and four from theirs. He worked construction during the day and had been working night shifts as a Safeway cab driver for over a year. The photo of Van Ness that accompanies news articles about his murder shows a broadly smiling middle-aged man with a gray handlebar mustache and tinted glasses. He's wearing a newsboy beret with a slanted bill, a white shirt, dark tie, and suspenders. His was a familiar face to employees and patrons of the Smoke Pit; when Carey saw him, he said, "Donny, that's the one." At 2:05 AM the brothers climbed into Van Ness's black-and-white cab and told him to take them to Dam Site Sixteen at Standing Bear Lake, a new park in northwest Omaha. Supposedly, they were going to meet friends to fish and drink beer. Van Ness didn't know the area and asked the dispatcher and a couple of fishermen for directions. At Carey's trial, the fishermen would identify him as Van Ness's passenger.

Carey's plan was to rob Van Ness, leave him at the lake, and steal his car. When asked at his April 1980 trial if he'd planned to shoot Van Ness, Carey replied, "I'm not sure whether or not I'd go through with it, but that was on my mind, yes." When Van Ness stopped the cab, Carey pointed his gun at the back of the driver's head and asked him for his money. Unexpectedly, Van Ness turned around and grabbed the gun. "I knew 'somehow' I had to shoot this man and as it turned out he reached back trying to take the gun from me as it fired and kept firing 3 or 4 shots" (July 14, 2018). Carey shot Van Ness twice in his head, once near his spine, and again in his hand. The burns on Van Ness's hand indicate that he'd been reaching for the gun when Carey fired it. "After I killed Van Ness, the gun was firing and then I heard this man say, 'Okay, okay, I quit!' [...] Seriously, to this day, I hear his words, 'Okay, okay, I quite [sic].' I don't think I will ever forget those words" (July 14, 2018).

In his telling of this story, Carey gives agency to the gun, and he speaks as if it is firing by itself. This could be read as an abdication of responsibility, but his culpability is something that he never denied. More likely, it's a testament to how little control he felt he had. On many occasions, Carey stressed that Donald thought that they were only going to commit a robbery, not murder. Involving his brother, who would be convicted of second-degree murder and serve twenty-eight years in prison, caused him guilt and anguish for the rest of his life.

While Donald pulled the body from the cab and laid it on the ground, Carey mopped up the blood. Donald, who at fourteen couldn't have been an experienced driver, drove them back to Omaha while Carey wiped their fingerprints from the backseat. They parked the cab, split the money that they'd taken from Van Ness, and walked to their mother's apartment. John and Ellen Douglas, who'd been fishing at the lake, later found Van Ness's body in the middle of the road. Ellen telephoned the police, who estimated the time of death at about 6:30 AM. A spent cartridge was found near Van Ness's body; his shoe was missing, probably caught on the door when Donald had dragged his body from the cab. That day, an article appeared in the *Omaha World-Herald*: "Clues Sought in Murder." On August 23, an artist's sketch of Carey and Donald, who were described as two clean-shaven men in their early twenties, appeared in the newspaper.

Carey and I ran out of time before I could ask and receive answers to all my questions. How had he and Donald spent their time after the murder? Did they replay the crimes in their minds? Did they create alibis? Did they spend the money (from $70 to as much as $140 or $150, depending on the source), and if so, on what? Did they hide? Pray? Watch the news coverage of their crimes or read about them in the paper with fear, pride, shame, shock, regret, or revulsion? How did they feel when they saw photos of Van Ness, who now had a name, a history, and a family? Did their mother suspect anything? Did they worry for her safety or continued employment, since she, too, was a cabbie and her sons, the robbers and killers of a cab driver? If she expressed fear about going to work, what did they say to her? And what led Carey to plan another robbery and murder, this one to be carried out alone?

On August 27, Carey hung around the taxi stand at the Greyhound bus depot at Eighteenth and Farnam, watching for another older driver. He was shocked when the first cab to respond to his call was driven by his forty-nine-year-old mother. I wondered if, for a moment, he took this as a sign that he should cancel his plan for the evening. He told his mother that he wanted a ride home, which she provided. Perhaps she didn't suspect anything. Or perhaps she sensed that by showing up when she did, she'd saved her son from some trouble that she couldn't pinpoint but whose gathering force she felt. Regardless, when Carey returned to the bus depot, he noticed a cab with an older driver parked outside of the depot. There were no other cabs around, which decreased the odds of someone identifying Carey as the perpetrator of whatever ensued. The driver, Maynard D. Helgeland, was a forty-seven-year-old Korean War veteran, a former boxer and construction worker, a divorcé, and the father of a daughter and two sons, the youngest of whom lived with his mother and stepfather in Wisconsin. The photo of Helgeland that accompanies newspaper articles about his murder show an attractive, clean-shaven man with a slim, rather athletic-looking body, short dark hair, and a serious expression. According to a 2018 article in the *Lincoln Journal Star*, Helgeland passed out drunk in his car on a winter night that was so bitterly cold, the doctors had to amputate his "severely frostbitten" feet as a result. But here, he is not yet an amputee and crouches, his hands crossed in front of him. He appears to be in his late thirties. He wears a short-sleeved, white knit shirt and white pants.

At the time of his murder, Helgeland had been sober for one year and had been driving a Happy Cab—something that a man with two prosthetic limbs could do to support himself—since July 2. Often, he and his oldest child, Kenny, who lived with him, drove the cab together. But on August 27, Kenny had gone to the horse races in Lincoln with a friend. That night, his father drove the cab alone. Carey told Helgeland to take him to the Benson neighborhood in north Omaha. When asked why he didn't shoot Helgeland in Benson, Carey answered, "I was too scared. I couldn't get it on my nerve yet." And so, he told Helgeland to take him back downtown.

In my rush to get as much information as I could about the murders, I failed to ask what happened between the time that Carey entered the cab (Did the two of them make small talk? Did Carey fidget and stutter? Did Helgeland seem to suspect anything?) and when he directed Helgeland to an alley near Twenty-Sixth Street and Dewey Avenue, just a few blocks from Carey's mother's apartment. There, he shot Helgeland three times in the head. Neighbors reported hearing shots, and some saw the cab and two men. "I told him to park, and then the second he turned around, that's when I fired the gun," Carey said in his confession. He pushed Helgeland out of the driver's seat and drove the cab to Twenty-Second and Leavenworth Streets. There, he searched Helgeland's pockets for money, but they were so blood-soaked that he gave up and left empty-handed (July 14, 2018). According to the August 31, 1979, edition of the *Omaha World-Herald*, Carey took Donald to see Helgeland's body to prove that he could kill a man by himself, though Carey said nothing to me about this. At his trial, Carey said that he took Donald to see the body "to get it off my chest." The police found Helgeland in his cab the next morning.

A few days after the second murder, Carey left town. "There was a girl ([ "Becky"]) we knew who needed to go someplace in Iowa, I forget where, but for some odd reason we decided it was simply the right time to get away for a couple days from all the heat and try to relax a little, so we decided to take [Becky] to someplace in Iowa" (July 14, 2018). Carey's use of the plural pronoun "we" suggests that Donald went on the trip, too, though that is not the case. In preparation for the trip, Carey stole a red 1978 Mercury station wagon from McFayden's Ford on South Twentieth Street.

After leaving Becky at her destination, Carey was driving on a highway near Charles City, Iowa, about 280 miles northeast of Omaha. A state trooper clocked him going sixty-nine miles per hour and gave chase. Carey stopped a short distance later. At that moment, he realized that he had a choice:

> I hid the gun beneath the driver's seat, I could have shot (and killed?) the Highway Patrolman who stopped me and who walked up to the door but I felt so tired; if I would had killed him then, drove back to Omaha, than [sic] what? If I wouldn't

had [sic] been stopped, went back to Omaha, then what? Would more killings continue? Would I become hardened to it? Would I like it? Over the years, those questions have crept into my thoughts (July 3, 2018).

Running the license plate revealed that the car was stolen, so the trooper arrested Carey for auto theft and for driving without a license. He didn't resist. And when the officers who secured the stolen car found a loaded .32 automatic pistol beneath the front seat and twelve .32-caliber cartridges in a paper bag in the back seat, they charged him with possession of an unlicensed firearm. Because the recent murders had been committed with the same type of gun, they suspected a link between Carey and those murders. Iowa authorities contacted the Omaha Police Department, and on August 30, Carey gave his confession to Omaha detectives Jack O'Donnell and Greg Thompson while in custody at the Floyd County jail. On the same day, Donald was interviewed at the Douglas County Youth Center in Omaha. Carey waived extradition and was transported to the Douglas County jail in Omaha on Friday, August 31.

The news of the murders was devastating for Carey's mother. The August 31, 1979 *Omaha World-Herald* presents three photos of her, a plump woman with her hair pulled back, sitting in a lawn chair, weeping and blotting her eyes with a handkerchief. It reports that her first tears were in sympathy for the two cabdrivers, slain for a few bucks. Next, she cried "tears of pain" when she learned that her sons had been arrested for the crimes. Finally, she cried "tears of anger" when she learned that Carey had purchased that gun from the man with whom she shared her cab. The photo is captioned "Mother of suspect . . . 'crying for everybody.'" I cannot imagine the depth of her anguish.

Just days before Carey's execution, his brother Dave told the *Lincoln Journal Star* that he was in prison for theft in Washington State when he learned that his twin had murdered two people. "I was shocked and yet I wasn't shocked. We both had a sensation that there was something or somebody coming after us. Me? I took off. But Dean decided to stay around, and he ended up serving a lot more time" (August 3, 2018).

Carey dismissed the idea that his harsh and violent upbringing excused his crimes. In the 2011 interview with Corey Matteson, he said, "When I killed the two men, that was my responsibility, my fault," he said. "The devil didn't make me do it. That was just me."

There are scant published details about how the Van Ness family received the news of Reuel's death. The *Lincoln Journal Star* reported that on the day of his stepfather's murder, then nineteen-year-old Tom Rinabarger and his mother awakened quite early, which he found odd at the time. He believes that they knew then that Reuel had been killed. Rinabarger learned that after picking up the Moore brothers, his stepfather had called the cab company dispatcher several times to ask for directions. Rinabarger is convinced that his stepfather was nervous about this fare and was trying to let dispatchers know his location. "He didn't need directions," Rinaberger said.

The Helgeland children have spoken often with the press about their father's murder and their feelings about Carey. Each has spoken of where they were and what they were doing when they received the shattering news of their father's death. Kenny, who had gone to the races on the evening of August 27, knew that something was wrong when his father didn't come home from work. The next morning, two officers arrived to tell him that his father had been murdered. At the time of her father's murder, nineteen-year-old Lori Helgeland (now Helgeland-Renken) worked as a cashier at Sapp Brothers, a truck stop and gas station in Council Bluffs, Iowa, just across the Missouri River from Omaha. An Omaha police detective telephoned her and asked her to meet him in the parking lot at the nearby high school. Helgeland-Renken took her best friend with her, and as they sat in the back of a police cruiser, the detective told them what had happened to her father.

Thirteen-year-old Steve Helgeland, who was living in Wisconsin with his mother and stepfather, was called out of class to receive the news, according to the February 5, 2018, *Omaha World-Herald*. He and his mother drove back to Omaha. There, he saw news footage of his father's covered body being wheeled away on a gurney from the crime scene. In 2011, Steve told Cory Matteson that because he'd been living in Wisconsin with his mother ever since his parents had divorced, "I've never had the opportunity to know who my father is." And on August 27, 1979, it was lost forever.

Those whose loved ones are murdered are known by many names: "survivors of homicide victims," "co-victims," and "survivors of violent loss." Theirs are heartbreaking stories of anger, vulnerability, fear, and trauma. Co-victims face all the common aftermaths of the death of a loved one—making funeral arrangements, notifying others, managing financial and legal affairs, and grieving. But because these particular deaths were so violent and unexpected, they have even more tasks to manage, such as identifying the body and making funeral arrangements, which can be particularly difficult when there has been physical trauma to the deceased—gunshots to the head, for example. And, too, they were expected to be involved with the murder investigation and to answer questions from the media.

Members of the Helgeland family made it clear to the press that what they most wanted was not to see or hear anything else about Carey Dean Moore. This, they said, could be achieved either through execution or by keeping him locked up. As Carey's 2018 execution approached, Lori Helgeland-Renken told *Omaha World-Herald* reporters Andrew J. Nelson and Joe Duggan that "It's been just exactly like it happened. I've had a lot of anxiety. I've decided I can't change the outcome of anything . . . so I just can't be immersed in it," meaning, perhaps, that with all the news coverage, it was as if her father had just been murdered again. If the execution of her father's killer was delayed yet again, Helgeland-Renken said that she'd prefer that the death sentence be changed to life in prison without parole. Then, she wouldn't have to hear about Moore in the news or legal battles over capital punishment.

For many years, when I saw how the Helgelands felt about my friend, I wanted to say, "But you don't know what he's like now. He's changed! He's not the same person that he was at twenty-one, when he took your father's life. He's more than a murderer." But those articles about the Helgelands, who *only* knew Carey Dean Moore as a murderer, remind me that my vision of this man was limited, too.

In 1974, five years before Carey killed two men, I moved to Iowa City to study music at the University of Iowa. But my academic career was lackluster: I never failed to clock into a waitressing shift at the Robin Hood Room, a restaurant in the mall, but I was so negligent about going to classes, practicing, and turning in assignments that I was placed on academic probation. By 1978, I was partying too many nights each week and only pretending to be a student. I was treading water, biding my time, though for what, I didn't know. It became clear that I had neither the discipline nor the passion for becoming a professional musician. But what was my passion, I wondered? I had worked a series of low-skill, low-paying jobs in florists, nursing homes, bars, and restaurants. I'd moved so many times that too often, I awakened at night in a panic because I didn't know where I was. Life had swept me up, and I was afraid of the direction it was carrying me. I felt like a failure.

That December, I visited my parents' home near Burlington, Iowa for the holidays and decided to remain there rather than return to my life in Iowa City. I found a full-time job tending bar at a working-class neighborhood tavern and saved enough money to buy my first car, a bile-green 1970 Camaro. After I got off work in the earliest hours of the morning, the other night bartender and I would go drinking and dancing across the Mississippi in Gulfport, Illinois, where the bars didn't close until 5:00 AM. On those days, I'd sometimes arrive home at about the same time that my father was getting up for his shift at the railroad. Other nights, I'd go straight home from work, cook supper, drink a few beers, and read—E. L. Doctorow, Erica Jong, Saul Bellow, Graham Greene, Shirley Ann Grau, William Styron, John Cheever, Bernard Malamud—until I fell asleep. But after several months of earning little more than minimum wage, reading to escape, and killing time by wandering around the rather new mall until I reported to work at 5:00 PM, I was bored and restless. I signed up for a summer session class, Journalism I, at Iowa Wesleyan College in Mount Pleasant, a twenty-five-mile drive from home. I loved having something to think about beyond my future at the tavern once business tapered off at the end of softball season or what a trial it was to live with my parents after being on my own in a vibrant college town. I thought often about the latter. No matter how much I loved dancing to "Do You Think I'm Sexy?" or how poignant I found Waylon Jennings's "Amanda," I was bored with the local disco and country-western scenes and missed the live jazz, folk, country rock, bluegrass, and even the punk that I'd enjoyed in Iowa City. I, who had developed a taste for the Ingmar Bergman and Jean Cocteau films I saw at the Bijou, the university theater, despaired of ever seeing a good movie again since Clint Eastwood's corny, cartoonish *Every Which Way but Loose* occupied one of Burlington's two movie theaters for an entire summer. What if I had to spend the rest of my life in such a small, limited place?

I aced the journalism class; and in August 1979, I enrolled as a full-time English and education major. My parents had paid for my first try at college, but I was picking up the tab for my second attempt. About the same time that my classes began, Carey murdered two men, and the families of Maynard Helgeland and Reuel Van Ness Jr. received the news that would forever change their lives. That fall, as Carey was sitting in the Douglas County jail, charged with two counts of first-degree murder, I was tending bar several evenings per week at the Holiday Inn and taking classes during the day—Shakespeare's Comedies, History of England I, Early American Literature, and Composition II. Between work, classes, and studying, I slept little. Given my record at the University of Iowa, I had such low expectations for myself that I didn't let myself dream of graduating. But I couldn't help myself: I was excited and relieved to be working toward something more ambitious than an eventual move from second to first shift at the tavern. Perhaps I would become a teacher, like my mother. Perhaps I'd move away and live in a big city.

I was grateful, then and now, for this second chance. Even though I was in my early twenties and had squandered the four years of tuition, room, and board my parents had provided, they gave me a place to stay and food to eat. They even loaned me a car and drove me to and from work until I had saved enough to buy my own. Iowa Wesleyan College had accepted me despite my abysmal GPA, and I easily made the dean's list every semester. When I couldn't take out the second loan I needed to pay my tuition and graduate in May 1981, my grandparents, who lived in a tiny aluminum mobile home in my parents' backyard, gave me the money from their meager savings account. They said it was a gift, but I paid back every penny.

I'm grateful that I had those several years in limbo. Because I didn't have to assume full adult responsibilities, I had the luxury of reading promiscuously and journaling about my angsts and dreams. I had the time to study and debate current events (the Farm Crisis during which a record number of Iowa farmers died by suicide, the plight of the Vietnamese boat people, the IRA bombings, the Americans taken hostage in Iran, the Three Mile Island nuclear disaster, the forward-thinking but ill-fated Equal Rights Amendment) so that I could determine what I believed and build a fledgling identity. Was I a union Democrat like my parents? Something further left? Something unclassifiable? I wasn't an atheist or an agnostic. But what type of theist was I? Was I to be conventional and conforming or a free spirit, an artistic type?

While Carey sat in jail preparing for his capital case in early 1980, I completed a four-week practicum at Horace Mann Middle School in Burlington. Mostly, I gave spelling tests, graded papers, and created bulletin board displays. But I liked working with the kids and knew that I wanted to be a teacher. On April 7, when I was in the home stretch of a semester that included the courses Shakespeare's Tragedies, History of England II, Educational Psychology, and American Literature II, I was starting to believe, really believe, that I would graduate from college. On April 7, Carey, believing that a trial court would be less likely to hand down a death sentence and so, waived his right to a jury trial, was convicted of two counts of first-degree murder in Douglas County District Court. On May 22, when I was tending bar at the Eagles Club a couple of days a week and awaiting the start of the summer session when I'd be enrolled in Developmental Psychology and Adolescent Literature, Carey's sentencing hearing was held. On June 20, when I was deep into Piaget's stages of cognitive development and Salinger's *Catcher in the Rye*, the panel sentenced him to death by electrocution on each of two counts of first-degree murder and set his execution date for September 20 at 6:00 AM—the first of many such dates.

In May 1981, almost seven years after I graduated from high school, I completed a degree in English and a certification to teach secondary English at Iowa Wesleyan College. Even though some of my friends from high school already had degrees, professions, marriages, houses, and children, I felt triumphant and was so very relieved to finally be a college graduate. Of the dozens of teaching positions that I'd applied for in a tight job market, I was offered two: one at a high school in tiny Morning Sun, Iowa, not far from home; and one at a large high school in faraway Omaha. At the Morning Sun high school, I would have been the entire English department and saddled with a half dozen new preps and the responsibility of running the school musical, a ghastly workload. The Omaha job required two new class preps, and I would live in what to me was a big, bustling, diverse city. By the time I was preparing to move to Omaha in August, Carey had been on death row for over a year. He and the families of his many victims were just days away from the second anniversary of the murders.

# 4

# "What Is Death Row Like?"

In my recurrent nightmare, I've been locked up for a crime that I didn't commit, and I'm powerless to change it. I live in an old-fashioned cell with a wall of bars, like those on *The Andy Griffith Show*. I can see and be seen; if I yell, I can be heard; if I want out, I can grab the keys hanging just outside and unlock the door. In one dream, I've even painted the walls lavender and decorated the room with a rag rug, a rocking chair, and a quilt. But I can't leave, can't see my kids or parents; and for that reason, even this pretty, relatively spacious cell is unbearable. One version of this nightmare features guards who are cruel and arbitrary. In others, I'm forced to live with several inmates, whose menacing presences overwhelm me as we sit elbow-to-elbow in a crowded dining hall or share a room packed with bunk beds. I'm terrified of what these people might do to me; and as an introvert, I grow anxious just at the thought of having to live so closely with so many strangers. And yet, the thought of solitary confinement and the paranoia, panic attacks, and hallucinations that might often result from such prolonged isolation terrifies me so much more. In the scariest version of all, I'm awaiting execution. Here, there's no chance of escape and no one to advocate for me, though in one dream, my mother tried to save me.

These dreams began in my early thirties, before I became involved in opposing the death penalty. Perhaps my nightmare was inspired by news reports about the state of the US judicial and penal systems. Or perhaps it was inspired by my concerns about metaphorical entrapment, imprisonment, and freedom. Fortunately, in the past decade or so, it's become less frequent. But it was never far from my mind in my thoughts about or interactions with

Carey. He admitted to his crimes and wasn't wrongfully convicted. Even so, he lived something terribly close to my nightmare for almost four decades.

The living conditions that Carey described are nothing like those of *The Andy Griffith Show*. I haven't seen the death row gallery at TSCI, where he lived from 2002 to 2018. But if it's anything like the typical maximum-security prison, the walls are concrete, with narrow windows. The steel doors are electronically controlled and have two hatches: one for viewing prisoners, and another for feeding them. The bed is probably a thin mattress on a ledge or steel bedstead. Carey described his living space as a "Cell and shower area size maybe 9' by 18', plus 4' by 5' attached mini-yard that has an iron-grate & door for air flow [. . .]. Beside[s] a bed, steele [sic] toilet/sink, in our cell, we also have a top bunk that we use as a shelf—the guys in the hole does [sic] not have this" (July 20, 2018).

Carey wrote often about what is variously called solitary confinement, administrative segregation, and restrictive housing (he called it "the hole"), a place he despised because it was far more confining than life in even the death row cells. He only described the hole's cells as being "smaller"—seven feet by twelve feet and seven inches, according to a 2017 report by Doug Koebernick, the inspector general of the Nebraska Department of Correctional Service (NDCS). Far from being forced to live with other inmates, as in my nightmares, when my friend was sent to solitary confinement, he was isolated as many as twenty-three hours per day. Personal property was prohibited. His recreational time was spent in a cage, a concrete yard surrounded by chain link fencing. Those who were in solitary confinement went to the yard alone, but death row inmates who were housed in segregation for what Carey described as administrative convenience (as opposed to disciplinary action) went two at a time, which allowed for some human contact. Carey hated the yard, "but one cannot stay locked up 24 hours a day" (January 15, 2003).

When I met Carey, I knew almost nothing about the living conditions on death row. I didn't know, for instance, that my friend had to submit to a body cavity search before and after he entered the visiting room and after he used the restroom nearby. Even when I attended the death row Bible study at TSCI several years later, I still found the security-related practices of a medium- and maximum-security prison unsettling: the unexplained delays when we checked in or out or waited for the inmates to arrive; the claustrophobic walk through the long, windowless, underground hallway from the gatehouse to the visiting room; the pat-down after I used the restroom. With each visit, my nightmares flashed before me; and when I left the prison after the check-out procedure, I felt giddy and so very grateful that the locked doors were behind me. Carey endured all this because he valued his relationships with visitors and the precious break that each visit offered from the tedium of prison. But how would I survive being locked up under such conditions?

"You said I could ask you any questions and so I will," I wrote in my third letter to Carey. "I am curious what it is like to be on Death Row. It is an experience that I cannot imagine. What are your joys and sorrows? Tell me as much as you want" (June 19, 1995). Some of my questions (what was it like to live in such a tiny space? What personal items could he have? Did he have any choice about what he ate and how often he got to go outside?) were easily answered. But others needed more complex answers. How did he endure the lack of privacy, autonomy, or meaningful work? How did he endure being separated from loved ones and the extremely limited opportunities for a physically and emotionally intimate relationship, if he'd had one at all? How did he endure the psychic burden of being locked up for all but a few hours per day with murderers? A study of the life histories of forty-three death row inmates, published by the American Psychological Association in 2007, found that 94 percent of the participants had been physically abused, 59 percent had been sexually abused, and 83 percent had witnessed violence in adolescence. It's no wonder that Carey wrote so frequently about conflicts between inmates. Like him, many of them had been badly broken by violent or abusive childhoods and poverty. On top of that, if the men on Nebraska's death row reflect the national average, at least 20 percent of them have a serious mental illness, according to Mental Health America.

On June 23, 1995, Carey wrote about his daily life at the penitentiary in Lincoln, where he'd lived since 1980. It was a less restrictive environment than what he would experience after the 2002 move to the prison in Tecumseh. Breakfast for those on death row was served around 6:40 AM, lunch at 11:15 AM, and dinner at about 4:30 PM. They were allowed to eat in the dining room, which was on a different floor from their cells. Most weekday mornings, Carey went to the prison's law library from 8:45 to 9:45 AM, where he practiced his typing. Then death row had its recreational time in the gymnasium or outside, in the yard: "Yard time is from 1:30 to 3:30 PM in a fenced-in area connected to the Death Row building—Unit 4."

In this and other letters, Carey wrote about the enduring, sustaining friendships he'd made, as well as the outbursts of frustration and violence among inmates due in part to the dysfunction in the Nebraska criminal justice system; the loss of friends and enemies to executions, resentencings, death by natural causes, and death by suicide; the adjustments required by the arrival of new people on death row; the long battle to gain contact visits with Dave; decisions about inmate conduct by the prison's disciplinary court; the quality of the food; the problems with understaffing; and the overuse of solitary confinement. In some letters, he barely mentioned any of these matters, but in others, he delved in and wrote at length.

When I shared details about my life, I was acutely aware of the sharp differences in our circumstances. Financially, the leanest period in my life (and the one that I wrote to him about in the most detail) followed my 1998 resignation from my position at Southern Illinois University—a job with good pay and benefits—so I could return to Lincoln and create a better child custody arrangement for my daughter and me. I paid a high price for this move: in my new life as an underpaid, part-time adjunct instructor at a private college and a part-time substitute teacher in the public schools, I never knew how much money I'd earn from one month to the next or if I'd even be employed the next semester. My income was so low that my children qualified for reduced prices on their school lunches (though we didn't take this benefit), and my parents often helped me out with unexpected bills. Since neither of my jobs provided health insurance, I paid handsomely for a practically useless commercial insurance policy for myself. Fortunately, my daughter had medical and dental insurance through her father, and my son was covered through the Nebraska Children's Health Insurance Program—Medicaid. But what did I have to complain about? I had made the *choice* to resign from a tenure track position so that I could return home.

After seven years of "not enough," I took a position at the University of Nebraska Omaha, which provided reliable paychecks, a retirement plan, and real health insurance. But even during my leanest time, I could cook whatever I wanted for dinner and shower when I felt like it. I could keep company with whomever I wanted, go to church whenever I wanted, and paint my walls in whatever color caught my fancy. If I wanted to get out of town, I could get in my car or board a plane. When my parents were dying of cancer, I was able to visit, help with their care, participate in their memorial services, attend to their personal effects. I had so much compared to my friend. The longer Carey and I knew each other, the more opportunities opened to me and the more secure my finances became. But on his end, the physical and monetary aspects of his life only became more restricted. Sometimes I felt like apologizing for living so well even as so much—both within and beyond my friend's control—went wrong for him.

I've read letters to the editors of various newspapers in which people complain about their tax dollars funding the "cushy" lives of those in prison. A free room and three square meals a day. Free cable TV. Free medical care. No taxes, insurance, or car or house repairs. A life of leisure, they say. But prison life can be expensive, with few opportunities to earn enough money to buy what one needs from the canteen or commissary, such as personal hygiene products, over-the-counter medications, postage, typing supplies, socks, boxers, and food.

Carey's opportunities to earn money were quite limited. Death row inmates were split into three groups. One group would clean the hall, dayroom, and shower for an entire month, earning "around $68–$69." For the next two months, they received ten dollars per month while they waited to clean again (June 14, 2008). Sometimes Carey was enterprising: he'd exchange canteen items for stamped envelopes to get "an extra 10 stamped envelopes free" (October 15, 2015) and entered sweepstake contests, though he never won. But if he didn't seek help from his family and friends, he had to do without. This was a challenging situation for me, as I'd never had a friend who appealed to me for money. Moreover, I'm dominated by the scarcity mentality that tells me to hang onto what I have, be it money, companionship, or food, because it's certain to run out too soon. When Carey asked me to help him buy food from the canteen, replace a broken television set, or buy a new Bible, my first thought was something that I might have said to my children when they asked for something: "Are you eating everything on your tray in the cafeteria?"; "Can't you find someone there to fix it for you?"; "Those don't wear out, you know." As with my children, I gave, but not easily or naturally.

Sometimes, Carey wanted something specific ("Please order me a 'Clown' 2018 calendar. Really ☺"). Right before one of his execution dates, he gave away his TV, CD player, typewriter, and radio. Some of these were returned to him when his execution was stayed, but what wasn't had to be bought with help from his friends. Once, he appealed to several of his supporters for regular financial assistance—twenty to thirty dollars or whatever we could spare every three months or so. It was difficult for him, and when he did ask, he always qualified his request by naming an expense that he knew I was facing (a new furnace, a medical test, all those trips to see my parents when they were sick and dying) and assured me that if I couldn't contribute, he'd understand. Carey kept careful accounts of the money and gifts he received. On January 10, 2014, he thanked me for sending him forty dollars for a new typewriter and updated me on his efforts to buy one. "I am still $25 away from the total of $173.41 needed to buy a Typewriter through the prison. So close! I received $50 from George Eisele, thank God, which went toward paying for a Typewriter."

Some gifts came with strings attached. When one friend who was sending him a hundred dollars a month learned that Carey was stopping his legal appeals in 2007, he gave him an ultimatum: "If I don't start up my appeals

[. . .] he would stop sending me money, stop accepting my phone calls, and stop writing to me. I didn't care about any of that!" (June 20, 2018). Carey stood his ground; the friend stopped sending money. Years later, the former benefactor apologized.

One need that our contributions couldn't satisfy was denied or inadequate medical care. In 2017, the American Civil Liberties Union and several other groups filed a lawsuit alleging that Nebraska state officials had failed to provide inmates with adequate medical and mental health care, a problem that was worsened by overcrowding and staffing shortages, and that the Nebraska Department of Correctional Services had failed to accommodate inmates "who are blind, deaf, hard of hearing, or have other disabilities" in accordance with the Americans with Disabilities Act. On June 8, 2020, a federal judge denied class-action status to the ACLU of Nebraska for this lawsuit.

Carey knew firsthand about the denial of medical care. While playing basketball in the early 1990s, he injured his knee, resulting in a torn anterior cruciate ligament. A surgeon placed two pins in his knee. On July 19, 2001, Carey wrote that X-rays showed that the pain he was experiencing was caused by one of the pins, which had come out partway. "For the past 2–3 years, I've been trying to get help on it," he wrote on March 2, 2007. "This place took me to Omaha maybe 6 months ago, but the Dr. refused to examine me; the only reason he gave was to say that he was the wrong Dr. for the job; so, I was brought back. The prison refused to do any more than that for me. (This influenced me a little about going to the Chair)." He would live with this condition for the rest of his life.

Still, he received what appears to have been adequate medical care for some problems. When he almost died from what may have been pneumonia in 2004, he spent six days at St. Elizabeth's Hospital in Lincoln and several more in the prison hospital. When he had trouble swallowing in 2014 due to a "potential neoplasm" and "a small sliding intermittent hiatal hernia," three guards and two highway patrolmen escorted him in handcuffs and shackles to the Tecumseh hospital, where a Lincoln doctor removed the blockage in his throat for testing (July 14). Carey didn't write about this again, so I don't know how it was resolved. When we each had shingles, also in 2014, we received the same antiviral medication. It wouldn't have occurred to me that the rash spreading on my chest in late June was shingles if Carey hadn't mentioned the condition in a couple of his letters a few months earlier. Even with the medication, which supposedly shortened the length and intensity of the outbreak, we had stories to share about our strange rashes, tenderness, tingling, and stabbing, scream-out-loud pain.

The list of inmates on Nebraska's death row is a changing cast of characters, ranging from as few as six—"Gosh, only six men!" (September 18, 2002)—to twelve at the time of Carey's execution, with Carey having been there longer than anyone else. He wrote about those who left death row through execution: Wili Otey, John Joubert, and his dear friend, Bob Williams. He wrote about those men—Charles Palmer, Roger Bjorklund, David Dunster, and Michael Ryan—who died of natural causes, and about Steven Harper, who died by suicide. He wrote about Randy Reeves, Mike Anderson, and Pete Hochstein, who left death row because they were resentenced to life in prison. "There is no way that I feel any jealousy & envy of Randy, Mike, or Pete. Glory be to God! They won! I wonder what kind of a future these men will have now," he wrote on September 18, 2001. When the charges against Jeremy Sheets, who spent four years on death row for the murder of seventeen-year-old Kenyatta Bush, were overturned and he was released, Carey wrote: "I'm glad he is out! But I just hope he is innocent!" (July 28, 2001). And he noted the arrival of new people. "Death Row should be gaining maybe 3 or 4 new guys due to the Norfolk bank robbery/murders; so we are all gearing up for that reality. I think a couple of us are dreading the new change" (February 7, 2004).

Unlike those of us in the "free world," those in prison can't pick who they live, work, or socialize with. Nor can they leave when spats explode into something more or when unresolvable conflict arises. Carey often wrote about these dynamics:

> Usually, most of us can get along with each other, which is a big surprise on account there are many fighting personalities now; in fact, Mike Ryan and one of the new guys got into a 3–4-minute fight maybe two weeks ago! (as a result, they were sent deeper into the hole for 45 days.) There is still a lot of stress and tension here, that seems never to leave any of us; I can't understand how others can deal with this place on a daily term without the Spirit of God living in their hearts (July 19, 2005).

Given the unrelenting stress and tension experienced by Carey and those he was living with, it's a wonder that he didn't devote even more space in his letters to the hostilities that resulted. I suspect that he wasn't telling me how often such outbursts occurred. When he did go into detail about a conflicted interaction, it was usually to tell me how he saw God speaking to him through it:

> Yesterday was a long day; I came in from death row yard a 1/2 hour early [. . .] and I forgot my t-shirt, at 3:30 one of the guys brought it in and asked me if it was mine, I said yes and he wiped his sweaty face on it; even though he was joking around, I felt he did wrong and without thinking I told him quite seriously, "If you want to disrespect me, I won't respect you." After this confrontation was over with, I asked God to help me handle times like that more appropriately . . . Well, the rest of the day was shot for me. You see, Lisa, I wasn't taught how to handle argumentative & stressful times, often I'd shy away if it's possible; now I'm trying to face arguments and conflicts, or life becomes extremely difficult. No kidding! Believe me, an argument can happen at the drop of a hat (in my opinion); gosh, I can't stand being in arguments (me or others), and more times than not it's over nonsense (June 23, 1995).

A coincidence that still astonishes me is that Roger Bjorklund, one of the other men on death row, had been a neighbor of mine in the early 1990s. My son and Roger's daughters had played together in the church parking lot that filled the block between their street and ours. The Bjorklund girls said that their dad worked in an electronics store. Their mother, whom I spoke to on several occasions, had an in-home daycare business. I only spoke with Roger once, and that was to inquire where our kids were. He didn't know. Not long after that, I ran into Mrs. Bjorklund at the grocery store. She was happy and excited about losing weight on a fruit diet and told me that they'd be moving soon, as Roger had found a better house for them than the one they were renting from the church. Not long after this meeting, I saw on the local news that Roger had been arrested and jailed for theft. A few months later, he was arrested for the kidnapping, rape, and murder of University of Nebraska–Lincoln student Candice Harms, crimes he committed with his friend, Scott Barney. I was shocked to learn that my son had played in the yard of a thief, kidnapper, rapist, and murderer. And it scared me to remember just how unremarkable Roger had seemed. After Roger's arrest, I wondered how his wife's home business had fared in light of her husband's crimes and the questions, stares, and whispers their daughters must have endured at school and beyond whenever people recognized them. In 1996, Mrs. Bjorklund divorced Roger and changed her family's unique last name.

Several times, Carey and I wrote to each other about Roger and his family. Carey wrote that Roger "hated Christians and always spoke bad of

God, Christians, and EVERYTHING between heaven & hell. [...] I did not know him that much, no one on the Row did. He was so full of hate & anger, Lisa. Really." But Carey understood why, given the difficult circumstances that Roger had experienced as a child. Carey said that sometimes, Roger wanted to give up on his appeals and be executed, but that he chose not to out of concern for his daughters.

Carey wrote about his conflicted encounters with Roger, again to demonstrate God's involvement in his life:

> I came that close to being in a fight with Roger Bjorkland yesterday during Death Row's yard. We were playing basketball and on opposite teams—he likes playing too aggressive for me and after losing my patience and a few words (no cussing), I couldn't take it any more. It got so bad and loud (arguing back & forth) between us that I thought we would be escorted off the yard & taken to the prison hole (lock up) for a couple weeks if not more, no exaggeration... But, they did not, thank God! Anyway, after I said "good morning" to him this morning after breakfast during shower, "he" apologized first and then I did and then "he" shook my hand (he initiated the apology and hand shake first); it's very hard for me to apologize or to forgive someone whether I am in the wrong or esp. when I am in the right... It's hard but "God" is busy working on me; thank God He is patient with us! ☺ (June 21, 1999)

On July 1, 2001, when Roger was thirty-nine, he died of a heart attack caused by undiagnosed diabetes and a blockage in his left and right coronary arteries, also undiagnosed. "I find it hard to accept that Roger Bjorklund died of a heart attack (blocked arteries leading to his heart)," Carey wrote on July 10. He may have been surprised by Roger's untimely death, or he may have wondered if Roger had died of another cause than that stated. "I hope and pray he was able to think about God during the hours before his death." Carey asked me to find an address for Roger's ex-wife so that he could send her his condolences.

Despite all these tensions, there were a few men that Carey counted as his closest friends. When the late Art Gales arrived on death row in 2001 after being sentenced to death for the murders of two children, he was celled next to Carey:

> If I have a "best friend" here, he is it. Art and I talked a lot then—and everyday [sic] since (except when we spent time in the hole); when he first came & when we first met, he cried so much, sharing how he was innocent and talking about the people he was

accused of hurting and killing; Lisa, he's innocent! I could feel his grief and sadness those years ago, and today. As I mentioned to him, I am thankful I am not in his shoes, innocent in prison. On a lighter side, we joke around often, lift weights together, when we have problems we share with the other and even if we can [sic] solve the problem, at least there's someone to talk to. We buy things at the canteen and share with each other, like ingredients for Burritos and Tuna wraps, and Marco Torres also joins with us; in fact Art, Marco, and myself are close [. . .]. Art [who is African American] and I have discussed so much, even about black and white issues. [. . .] When Art first joined us on the Row in 2001, I said to him that I did not know if he had ever served time in other prisons but if he ever needed someone to talk to than [sic] "I'll be there" to try to help.

If Art, Marco, and myself are speaking to each other and if something we say reminds us of a piece of a song, we would quickly sing that song like the above in quotation marks "I'll be there" by the Jackson's (December 17, 2009).

In 2002 when Carey was working at the food cart serving food to other death row inmates at the prison at TSCI, a spat erupted:

I happen to be serving Eggs at breakfast to Mike Ryan (who died of brain cancer in 2015 here) when he thought I hadn't served him enough eggs, he accused me and got in my face and immediately Art said right away, "Why don't you get in others faces like that when they serve you?" He quickly backed away. A friend like Art does that, I didn't have to say a word and Mike never again questioned the portions I has [sic] served him (July 20, 2018).

It wasn't only the other death row inmates that affected Carey's day-to-day well-being but the shortage of staff, the shortage of well-qualified staff in particular. On March 5, 2017, the *Omaha World-Herald* reported that TSCI had fifty-three unfilled vacancies, which means that to fill shifts the NDCS had to resort to mandatory overtime. That year, Scott Frakes, the director of the NDCS, announced $2,500 recruitment bonuses to be paid out quarterly for one year and retention initiatives in the form of merit pay based on years of service to ameliorate the problem caused by understaffing, inexperienced staff, exorbitant overtime expenses, and high employee turnover rates. The NDCS website lists the requirements for the position of corrections officer as a high school education or the equivalent, a valid driver's license, the ability to legally possess a firearm and ammunition, and that one be at least eighteen years of age. In Nebraska correctional officers can even be teenagers not long out of high school.

When I asked Carey if he was aware of understaffing or underqualified staff he wrote:

> No doubt, yes! For both questions. Sometimes we joke that some recent recruits [*sic*] was found on the railroad tracks or farmers & their wives! Some come only for a year or two, only a stepping stone for better things; some only stay a short period because administration wants them to be hardasses toward us when there's no reason, and a few tries to be super-cops for no reason and they run against someone who doesn't care anymore and the person hurts them bad and the administration cries foul [. . .]. In times past, they did their best not to inform press and the politicians but when there's a riot and fires and killings, well, how can they keep that a secret? I can't tell you many stories (June 14, 2018).

I didn't know if Carey didn't want to tell me about some matters because he thought they would upset me or if it was risky or dangerous for him to speak of them. Either way, I found it troubling whenever he alluded to one of these stories. On July 20, 2018, he wrote that "on a couple occasions" the life of one of his friends "has been in jeopardy which he and I have discussed." But because he didn't explain or offer an example, I was left imagining what he couldn't tell me.

Staff-related problems weren't new. In 2008, Carey wrote about a prison guard who tried to poison the water jugs that the death row inmates drank from with eye drops. Tetrahydrozoline, an ingredient in Visine, Clarine, Murine, and other eye drops, is a decongestant and vasoconstrictor.˙ If ingested, it can be absorbed through the gastrointestinal tract into the bloodstream and then travel to the heart and central nervous system, where it slows the heart rate and lowers the blood pressure to dangerous levels. It's the reason why you're supposed to contact a poison control center immediately after swallowing them. Carey wrote that when another guard reported the incident, the suspected poisoner was escorted out of the prison but wasn't arrested:

> We have been writing to our attorneys & senators about this; the guard hasn't been fired (yet) and is waiting for a possible hearing to decide what has been decided. Well, we shall see what will happen but we're trying to pour gas on the fire and wake people

up to what goes on in this super maximum-security prison (January 24, 2008).

Carey didn't mention the problem again, so I don't know if or how it was resolved. I've found no coverage of the incident in the news. In his essay, "Marion Prison," journalist Laurence Gonzales wrote, "Of all the powers that anyone has in the world over us, no one has the broad discretionary powers of a prison guard." What must it be like to be utterly dependent for your basic needs on the type of people who would poison your water supply? What if no one had noticed the attempted poisoning?

"This is a tough place," Carey wrote on July 28, 2017, "and all of us (staff and inmates) needs [sic] so much prayer."

Carey was sure to mention disruptions in his daily routine. John Lotter, Art Gales, and Marco Torres, the three men with whom Carey ate his meals, shared special holiday and birthday meals that they made with food from the canteen. These meals were expensive for Carey, but he chipped in what he could. "It's John Lotter's birthday today; Art Gales, Marco Torres, Lotter, and myself chipped in on making: Art's birthday 1st—burrito's; John's birthday—Tortilla chips & chili; and Tuna wraps (tortillas)" (May 30, 2016). And he wrote about rule changes and losses of privileges, some of which surprised me. "All the ironing boards/irons was taken out because they thought we'd use them as weapons against each other and on them (staff), so soon we'll be walking around in wrinkled clothing; we'll look like slobs or bums! Soon" (June 10, 2015). They'd had irons?

Barring a move to a new prison or an inmate's arrival to or departure from death row, Carey mused that "Life doesn't often change for us on death row unless we get further in the hole" (October 27, 2009). When he was taken in handcuffs and shackles to a hospital in Lincoln for knee surgery, he got a glimpse of what life beyond the prison was like. "The scenery was overwhelming, intoxicating, and rough on the nerves. I loved it!" (July 24, 2001). At an in-person meeting, I asked him to tell me about one remarkable thing that he'd seen on that journey. To my surprise, it was the playground equipment at a nearby school, how colorful it was. He'd never seen anything like that.

Occasionally, we wrote to each other about food. I'd share stories about my cooking disasters; the excellent fare at our church potlucks; something I'd made that actually turned out (iced butterhorn yeast rolls!); the homemade fudge, peanut brittle, and Swedish S cookies that my mother sent at Christmas; and Carey and Ian's love of hot sauce. Occasionally, he gave prison food a good review. "Christmas day, the entire prison was served double portions on everything for lunch, and it was the first time we had strawberry cheesecake—I was able to get 7–8 cheesecakes [by swapping his food with others]. No doubt, I have a sweet tooth! ☺ " (December 31, 1995). But he mostly found it unsatisfactory. "We had sloppy joe's for lunch today, and now (seven hours later), I am the only one with an upset stomach. So I skipped supper tonight (maybe 1 1/2 hours ago); but now, I am hungry (with still an upset stomach)" (October 4, 2002).

On November 23, 2001, he wrote to me while he waited for breakfast. "Maybe in half an hour, it will be time for breakfast (pancakes), I will skip—just coffee. I wish the prison served maple syrup but they do not, just plain (if I can call it plain)." And sometimes, he simply announced what was for lunch. "Chili mac!" Only once did he write about a food that he hadn't eaten since coming to prison and was longing for. When I mentioned that my dad had bought me a couple of rhubarb plants at the farmer's market, which he and my daughter planted, he lamented, "I haven't had any 'rhubarb' in over 24 years and I love rhubarb pie. 'Help me, Lord!!!'" (July 13, 2004). If I were limited to starchy, fatty prison cafeteria fare and packaged junk food from the canteen, I'd miss rhubarb and so much more—fresh green beans and corn on the cob, tree-ripened pears, kimchi, fresh ginger root tea, frozen yogurt and blueberries, curries, curries, and curries, my oatmeal pancakes slathered with peanut or almond butter, and my number one comfort food, a baked potato. I'd also miss choosing what I ate and when.

Despite the spirit-crushing tedium and stress of prison, the pleasantly unexpected arrived. "For a couple weeks now, the gallery we are on (Upper A) has a visiting field mouse (I assume it's from the field); it runs super fast & hops high! ☺ So now we can't keep any Canteen items in sacks on the floor. I had a chance to get it once but it's a hopper & it is fast! No luck: I'm hoping for another chance! ☺ So I set a little trap . . . 'Help me, Lord.' ☺ Do you like mice?" (April 19, 2016). I find them beautiful with their tiny pink ears, little black eyes, and delicate feet. But when one takes me by surprise or when I find one in a mousetrap that I've set in my garage come cold weather, I scream.

"The latest news about the mouse is that it ate through Ray Mata's guiter [sic] case or strap (I think case). I haven't seen or heard the mouse in a while, although no one is keeping anything on the floor; well, except for one person . . . Marco Torres has been sleeping on the floor, which he says it's great for his back!" (May 30, 2016). And that was the last I heard about it.

During Carey's last summer, I finally asked him about matters we'd never spoken about. One of those subjects was romantic relationships. Other than my early letters about my troubled relationships with my children's fathers, I had never written to him about the men with whom I'd kept company. Again, I didn't want to make him feel uncomfortable or less than fully human by reminding him that he'd seemingly lost any real opportunity to have something so necessary in his life.

At NSP, I'd seen that some death row inmates had visitors—local women, women from other states or even countries—who provided companionship and financial support. Some of these women had been with the inmate long before he was sentenced to death. But others were drawn to the celebrity (notoriety, really) of being with a man on death row and sought out such a relationship, in spite of—or perhaps because of—the limitations. On our part, there was never a suggestion from either Carey or me that ours was anything but a platonic friendship. I appreciated the freedom this allowed us.

"Why haven't you pursued a relationship with anyone?" I asked a little over a month before his execution. "Or why haven't women pursued romantic relationships with you—or have they?" Carey answered frankly. "I was only 22 when I came on the Row, and God as my witness I didn't ever want love to sneak in. I didn't want the hassles of caring, of loving, thinking about someone." But once, it happened. In the mid-1980s, "Jan," an old friend of Carey's, and her daughter "Kelly" began visiting him at NSP. Kelly, who was a few years younger than Carey, and her five- or six-year-old son lived with Jan in Omaha. "The 3 of us (Kelly, Jan, myself) had Bible study and talked a lot; at the end of Bible study, we would all hold hands [to pray] and then one day my heart began to beat faster & faster and I absolutely didn't want to feel love. No way. I was trying to deny it for a while, when Jan got up to do something, restroom maybe, and [Kelly] first said to me [omitted words]—faster heartbeat & sweaty hands. I admitted the same to her." For the next couple of months, Kelly and Carey wrote of their feelings for each other but kept their relationship a secret because Kelly knew that her mother wouldn't approve. "Bible class was one thing but love, no, I guess not." When Jan discovered that Carey and Kelly were in love, she stopped visiting. And because Kelly didn't drive, she could no longer come to Lincoln to see him. "I was saying to God 'This is why I didn't want to be in love or fall in love with someone because love hurts' and I think He said to me, 'At least you have a chance to love! At least you have a chance to grow!'" (July 13, 2018). Carey dealt with his disappointment and hurt by writing poems and prose pieces that he sent to Dave. He never allowed himself to love a woman in that way again.

# 5

# Whispers and Shouts

When I met Carey, he was thirty-eight and had long since become a mature Christian whose faith had been tested and tempered many times over. But it wasn't until I'd begun writing about our friendship during the last few months of his life that I realized that I didn't know the story of his conversion to Christianity. We'd told each other important pieces of our testimonies, but I don't recall either of us asking to hear the grand narrative of how the other had become a Christian. Nor did we feel the need to share those stories with each other.

Mine was hardly straightforward. I'd loved Methodist Sunday and Bible school as a child but was keenly interested in Judaism as a teenager and dreamed of converting. During my early and mid-twenties, I explored Hinduism and studied and taught ashtanga yoga in the 1980s, before Americanized yoga became so widespread. Ultimately, it was the insights about the mystical Christ from yogis and philosophers such as Paramahansa Yogananda, Baba Ram Dass, Joseph Chilton Pearce, and others that led me back to Christianity. When I was thirty-three, my pacifism and desire to belong some place brought me to the Church of the Brethren. Now, when I tell highlights of my spiritual autobiography, I include a long section about Carey Dean Moore, whom I count as one of my great teachers.

I had assumed that not long after Carey was sent to death row, he'd had a jailhouse conversion, an urgent grasp by a man in a dire situation for the solace and salvation found in the gospel. A January 29, 2008, letter suggested such timing:

> I love the Christian faith because each year "He" changes my understanding & urges it to grow and even mature a bit, even cutting away what is bad and harmful to me and to others. Amen! [...] I have been journeying with our Lord for nearly 30 years; I have barely scratched the surface of my faith and most especially the Bible whose knowledge is so vast & whose heart is so incredibly huge, Eph 3:14–21.

Carey wrote this when he was forty-nine, so something significant must have happened when he was in his late teens or early twenties. But what made it hard to pinpoint exactly when this had occurred is that in several letters, he referred to "a long countless list" of people who'd influenced his faith. When I praised him for having been instrumental in the transformation of a man on death row, he responded, "I don't know if I had something to do with ['Frank's'] conversion to Jesus Christ but, I like to humbly think that at the very least I helped a little." Then he told a story about hitchhiking to West Virginia when he was eighteen. On his way back to Nebraska, a preacher and his family gave him a ride and invited him to share a meal with them. When they weren't looking, Carey stole the wife's billfold from her purse. After he left their house, he threw away the billfold, identification cards, and photographs, pocketed the cash, and continued thumbing for rides. "The guilt from this and meeting this Christian couple influenced me years later to accept Jesus as my personal Savior! That was a drop of water in an ocean of witnesses who showed me His light" (October 27, 2009). So, he couldn't say precisely when his metanoia—his fundamental change of mind—had occurred because its seeds hadn't borne fruit until several years later.

Shortly after his arrest for the murders, Carey had "desperately" wanted to talk to someone, so he called the pastor of the Omaha church that he'd sometimes attended when he was home from reform school or one of his foster homes. "It was a church where I talked to God and felt some sort of a connection and a bond to its members (even though I thought most of them looked past me)" (December 5, 2002). Carey didn't name the church or the denomination; but I now wonder if it was the Church of Jesus Christ of Latter-day Saints that he'd attended with his father as a child, the church where he'd been baptized. In 1981, when Carey was twenty-three, he received a letter from "the Mormon Church" telling him that it had "kicked [him] out of their manmade church" because he had committed murder (July 9, 1995). But in 1979, while he awaited trial for the murders, I suspect that it was this pastor that he called for help. When the pastor visited, Carey could see that jail was "completely 'foreign' to him," and that he was so uncomfortable that he "mostly listened to me, said just a couple of words, and then he left very quickly!" Carey hoped the pastor would return, but it never happened. For the rest of his life, Carey would invite people into Christian communion with him. Only some would accept.

> However, Lisa, God brought just the right amount of spiritual medicine, even with other prisoners & staff, and of course His Spirit was there to help me every step of the way—whether down in the valley so low or even on top of the mountain top. You have no idea how many people God has put in my path, maybe even to stumble on . . . (I can't even count them all!) [. . .] I came to understand that GOD was sending people to me only when HE thought I needed "whatever I needed" (December 5, 2002).

I find it curious that some of those same people doubted his sincerity. The man who had been pastoring Carey when I met him in 1995 doubted that Carey was a true believer, which hurt him. One of the reasons that Carey refused to give interviews to the press was that once an article was published, he heard from readers who doubted his faith. Some thought that he was using Christianity for personal gain. Others thought that he needed proselytizing so that he could become a "real" Christian. I got a taste of this soon after his execution, when several asked me, "Was your friend really a Christian?" I told them that I'd never doubted that Carey was right with God and that his level of faith was what I aspired to. But once I was so exasperated with this question that I snapped, "Don't worry about Carey Dean Moore's Christianity. Worry about yours and that of the people you're sitting next to in church." It wasn't my finest moment; and yet through this encounter, I truly understood my friend's frustration.

At his memorial service, a few of the many who rose to speak about Carey claimed that he wouldn't have been a Christian if he hadn't come to death row. But that wasn't the story that he'd told me. He said that he had met God long before he murdered two people, which raises so many important questions. Had Carey considered himself a Christian when he'd killed those two people? And if so, how did he reconcile these different aspects of himself? Had he temporarily lapsed or backslid during that week in August 1979? Had his gradually growing faith in God's promises been too frail to withstand the temptations he was facing? Or did he have another explanation?

During the spring and summer of 2018, when I was hurrying to get as much essential information from Carey as I could before it was too late, I asked him to tell me about his conversion. Had it been as sudden, dramatic, and singular as that of Saul of Tarsus, who was so blasted by God's glory that he was struck blind and had to be led by the hand into Damascus?

Three days later, something like scales fell from his eyes, and he was Paul, a new man who became a follower of Jesus and aligned himself with those he had previously persecuted. Or had Carey's conversion been more like that of bold and fearful, loyal and betraying, believing and doubting Peter, who moved closer to God by degrees, two steps forward, one step back? In her collection of essays, *Traveling Mercies: Some Thoughts on Faith*, Anne Lamott writes, "My coming to faith did not start with a leap but rather a series of staggers from what seemed like one safe place to another." Lamott compared these landing places to lily pads: when she looked back at some of these early resting places, she could "see how flimsy and indirect a path they made. Yet each step brought me closer to the verdant pad of faith on which I somehow stay afloat today." Likewise, my own faith journey hadn't been the single, bold leap that I longed for, but a steady, incremental movement toward God, one-thirty-second of an inch per day—a seemingly inconsequential movement until I turned around and saw how far I'd come.

In the end, neither theory was true. A few weeks before his execution, Carey offered an entirely different metaphor to explain the evolution of his faith:

> Just before 4 am this morning I woke up and I couldn't get back to sleep because I couldn't stop thinking about your latest question: "how you transformed from one who killed two people to one of the most exemplary Christians I know." My humor wants to say to you that you must not know too many people! ☺ Just kidding, of course.
>
> When I woke up this morning and couldn't get back to sleep, I was recalling when was I saved? And I'd like to think that God whispered this thought to me, to look in His Word for the word 'whisper' because I felt like the answer was there . . . Read Job 26:14 (in part), 'how faint the whisper we hear of him!' Oh, that's awesome! I got up and read that just after 4 am!
>
> I was in a Omaha "Youth Center" for juveniles (along with Dave) many times from maybe 7 to 9 years old, just in & out for a couple months at a time; while there though, they had church service even during the week with hymn singing; there's a couple songs that I still remember today that we had sung: "Do Lord, Oh do Lord, oh do you remember me?" and well, a couple more of those songs spoke to me, I knew there was some sort of a Creator or Heavenly Father "up there." Did He "whisper" this to me beginning then? And now and then throughout my teen-years? I think so. But, most definitely, when I was 16, I was at YDC

(Youth Development Center) in Kearney, and listening to the Lutheran pastor really spoke to me; I felt so tired of struggling on my own, I felt depressed, angry all the time, I didn't want to fight any more, and I wanted to stop resisting Him; so I asked Jesus to come in to my heart and save me from my sins—past, present, and future. I asked Pastor David Cloeter to baptize me [this was actually Carey's second baptism], which of course he did; but of course, there was still that bad nature inside of me, wanted to get out . . . Naturally, I had one hand in hell and one hand in heaven, being pulled; I would hear His whispers and sometimes He shouted but I drowned Him out with things even though I was still asking for His strength! (July 10, 2018).

Carey's faith story was one of learning to better discern and magnify God's voice, whether he heard it as a whisper or a shout. In my mind's eye, I see Carey at a control panel, squelching down the world's clamor so that he can better hear God. More people than he could name appeared during his life to show him how. He, in turn, would teach and encourage others, including me, to do the same.

I spent the first forty-five years of my life in mainline Protestant churches that were light on prayer and Bible reading and heavy on social justice (feeding, clothing, and doctoring people, and opposing corrupt systems) and community-building social activities (ice cream socials in the park, providing and serving meals at a soup kitchen). Through these churches, I met good people, some of whom were or are my closest friends, and I became involved in worthy causes. But in these churches, it seemed that God was a concept to talk about rather than a living being one could have a relationship with. Although we had stimulating discussions about books like John Hick's *The Metaphor of God Incarnate*, John Shelby Spong's *Why Christianity Must Change or Die*, or Jim Wallis's *The Soul of Politics: Beyond "Religious Right" and "Secular Left,"* most people that I met in the more liberal or progressive churches seem puzzled by or even skeptical about the possibility that God might have something to say directly to ordinary people like them—us. Indeed, when I first met Carey, that was my position. But in time, I grew to crave direct, personal encounters with God. I wanted to hear God's voice as clearly as Carey did. And in time, God started speaking to me in a voice more felt than heard by the physical ear. As the voice began to impart its messages ("Stop fearing and step into your power." Or "Enlarge the place of your tent." Or even, "She knows what you're like, and she's forgiven you."), it confirmed its source and authenticity. I cannot explain any of this.

In 2000, four years after I met Carey, a time when I had much to worry about and was in dire need of spiritual support and guidance, I began attending a Pentecostal church while maintaining my ties to the social gospel tradition at the Church of the Brethren. At the Pentecostal church, I was taught by people who were committed to nurturing an intensely personal relationship with God through Bible study, prayer, and service, and I was baptized there by immersion after giving my public testimony. Because American Protestantism is now as deeply divided as our national politics, my ability to see something good and sustaining on both sides of the rift, the conservative evangelical and the liberal social gospel, is so unusual that I have yet to meet anyone else who also appreciates and practices both. It is a gift and a complexity for which I am grateful, but it has also complicated my life.

The Pentecostal church's teachings spoke directly to those aspects of my life that I wanted to change, like my unwillingness to forgive myself and others for not living up to my impossible standards or my tendency to worry obsessively rather than trusting my problems to God. I was grateful for the evangelical emphasis on the direct experience of God's presence and the dynamic work of the Holy Spirit in the individual, and I turned to this church because of what I'd seen in Carey's powerful and empowering spirituality. In part, this new desire was his gift to me.

Yet during the presidential election of 2008 and the early months of Obama's presidency, I found this church's political discourse (the congregants' more than the pastors') so irreconcilable with what Jesus taught that I had to leave. Though I missed their devotion to Scripture and prayer and continued to attend an occasional service or class there, I felt more at home, at least socially and politically, among the people in the liberal gospel tradition. All the while I felt like a misfit in such churches, spiritually and theologically. Over the next several years, I attended a couple of services each weekend at some combination of three social gospel churches—one Lutheran (ELCA), one United Methodist, one Church of the Brethren—and occasionally, the Pentecostal Church. Carey was critical of my "church-hopping" and what this behavior communicated to my children. He encouraged me to commit to just one, and when I finally did that in 2017, he rejoiced.

When I met Carey in 1996, he was a different type of Christian than I had known. He read the Bible daily and was saturated in its images, metaphors, tropes, and themes. His faith in God's promises was absolute, and he was certain that anything he needed—guidance, comfort, provocation, perspective, conviction, healing—would come to him through the Scripture, prayer, and Christian friendships. We both memorized Scripture. But when he told me that he was memorizing the 119th Psalm, the longest chapter in the Bible, I knew that he was running a marathon while I, with my pocketful of memorized verses from the Psalms and the Sermon on the Mount, was running a loop around my backyard. "If a person had only Psalm 119 and nothing else of the Bible, he or she could live faithfully and be fed spiritually by God for the rest of the person's life," Carey wrote on November 5, 2001. Later, he said with regret that he'd been filled with pride and ego when he told people that he was memorizing all 176 verses of that majestic psalm. Presenting himself as superior to others was long a concern of his. Early in our friendship, he wrote: "Will you let me know if at times it feels like I am 'preaching' to you about whatever?" (September 29, 1997). "Maybe a little," I wrote back. "But I don't mind. ☺"

For him, the Bible was, as the psalmist said, "a lamp for his feet and a light on his path" (Ps 119:105). Indeed, the wisdom and comfort he found there pushed back the heavy darkness of prison life and his guilt for having murdered two men and for having involved his half-brother in one of those crimes. But he preferred to think of Scripture as food, as in Psalm 119:108: "How sweet are your words to my taste! Sweeter than honey to my mouth!" He took pleasure in craving the Word ("It's wonderful being hungry, isn't it?" November 5, 2002) and professed that the Bible "fed" him in so many ways. And what a zesty appetite he had: "I am almost finished reading Acts, and soon will begin reading the 12 minor prophets in the Old Testament—beginning with Hosea and finishing with Malachi. I can hardly wait!!! ☺" (August 20, 2002). I laughed in delight at his excitement.

The Bible gave him intellectual food, as well. Even though his formal education had been frequently disrupted and, finally, cut short by trauma and frequent relocations, he was a surprisingly good writer and critical thinker. I suspect that he developed these abilities by reading, analyzing, and memorizing Scripture; writing letters to many and diverse correspondents; and completing the free Bible studies that he sent away for. "All last week I was busy doing two Bible courses, I must had done 10 to 12 bible lessons, which I mailed yesterday to both Bible course ministries" (September 16, 2002). He read little outside of the Bible, including books that I'd written and sent to him ("Anyway, Lisa, I am praying for your book! ☺" May 22, 2001). A few of the exceptions that I remember are Foxe's 1563 *Book of Martyrs*, Kathleen Norris's *Dakota: A Spiritual Geography*, and a book about deprogramming people in cults, which he asked me to buy for him. But he'd read the Bible over and over in an unbroken stream, from the first page of Genesis to the last page of Revelation. Sometimes, he attended to a couple of streams at once. "This morning I read Kgs. 1:28–53 & 2:1–12, and Mt.

13:1–22; I'm trying to read a chapter a day (except Sundays) more or less; I don't know what shape I would be in if 'Bibles' were prohibited in prison" (August 25, 2003).

Though he'd read everything in the Bible literally thousands of times, Carey always found something that spoke to him anew. When rereading Lamentations for the umpteenth time, his pleasure was like that of one savoring a delicious meal. When I told him that I was attending a group study on Job, he wrote, "The very first time I read this book [...] it really depressed me out, but each time after it has been doing just the opposite; that sure is surprising to me!" (January 13, 1999).

He also provided guidance when those of us in George Eisele's home Bible study were struggling with Romans:

> Romans is the toughest book to read and understand and it seems like most Christians can get twisted around certain verses or certain controversies [...]. What do you think??? You must remember, try not to feel intimidated while reading because we can read a book year after year (ect) [sic] and still discover new things. Amen! And just because we don't understand something one year, that doesn't mean the Holy Spirit won't reveal its meaning at another time (April 4, 2004).

He prayed many times a day with utter faith but took no personal credit for this act, or for the results. "It is the Holy Spirit urging me to speak to God and to listen to Him throughout the day" (October 21, 2003). Prayer was his gift to others. "I wake up in the night, and for some odd reason, the Holy Spirit makes me think of you, Ian, or Meredith. Really! ☺ So I pray for you before I fall asleep ☺" (December 4, 2001). I often thought about what a good pastor he would have made had he been able to go to seminary and been called to lead a church.

Carey liked to pose provocative questions for the two of us to debate. Sometimes we'd explore these theological issues over several letters. Did God hear and respond to the prayers of the Philistines? (October 6, 2007). "Why did 'God' choose a man like [King] Saul when later he'd break God's heart (which he knew all long [sic] ... )?" (July 26, 2002). How do our prayers change as we age? When people say that they're praying for guidance, is that really a way to avoid saying "yes" to a request? How does the use of gender-neutral pronouns, which I insisted upon to refer to God and people, change our understanding of some passages?

We had much larger disagreements about some of the applications or interpretations of Scripture. In a large part, this was because he usually had a literalistic interpretation of Scripture, while I believe that some passages require a more contextualist reading. One of the topics that he and I agreed to, in his words, "politely disagree about," was homosexuality. He took literally such verses as Leviticus 18:22, in which people of the same sex who lie together are "an abomination," or 1 Corinthians 6:2–11, which lists behaviors that will keep one from inheriting the kingdom of God, including greed, drunkenness, idolatry, and homosexuality.

The first time I visited Carey at the new prison in Tecumseh was in 2002. As Carey, George Eisele, and I were chatting over Pepsi and M&M's from the vending machines, I made a slight reference to the story of Sodom and Gomorrah. Carey said that we should look at that story together, and I silently chastised myself for even mentioning it. The exact nature of the sin that led to the destruction of these cities wasn't and still isn't clear to me. Was it homosexuality, even though that word wasn't coined until the nineteenth century and so wasn't mentioned in the Bible? Certainly, the intention of the men of Sodom is clear when they call out to Lot, "Where are the men who came to you tonight? Bring them out to us so that we can have sex with them" (Gen 19:5). Or was the sin a refusal to care for the poor? Ezekiel tried to shame the Israelites into repentance by telling them that their behavior was worse than that of the Sodomites: "Now this was the sin of your sister Sodom: She and her daughters were arrogant, overfed and unconcerned; they did not help the poor and needy. They were haughty and did detestable things before me. Therefore I did away with them as you have seen" (Ezek 16:49–50). Or was the sin inhospitality? The behavior of the Sodomites who surrounded Lot's house and demanded that he relinquish his guests so that they could rape them stands in sharp contrast to Lot's gracious hospitality, which includes preparing a feast for his guests. And, yet, how could anyone consider Lot righteous after he offered his virgin daughters to the rapists of Sodom in order to protect his guests from them? Carey was certain about the sin that led to the destruction of Sodom and Gomorrah; George and I were not.

At the time of that 2002 Bible study, I was already aware of Carey's position on homosexuality because his first letter to me on this topic was written on November 22, 1995, not long after we began corresponding. In Carbondale, my children and I attended a United Church of Christ whose congregation was "open and affirming" toward homosexuality. The pastor, whose son was gay, taught a class in queer theology. And when she moved away, the interim pastor was a woman who had been in a same-sex relationship that had spanned decades. Members of the LGBTQ community were

Sunday school teachers and involved in youth group leadership. Two male congregants were married in our sanctuary, and I was honored to serve cake at the reception that followed. My children and I often socialized with two congregants, both lesbians though not partnered to each other.

Carey's views were different:

> "I think it's great that they (gays) are going to church to hear about God's love, but, I think it's such a tragedy when people in the church (Christians) excuse the gays, and knowingly give permission for them to continue; we should give our best in faith to escape sin's grip upon our hearts. Don't you think so, too? I'm sure you do. Praise God Almighty! ☺"

I don't have a copy of the letter that I wrote in reply to this, but on January 2, 1996, Carey quoted a bit of my response: "You wrote: 'The Old Testament & the writings of Paul are pretty clearly against it [homosexuality], but Jesus said nothing on the subject. In fact, Jesus didn't have to say much about sex.' This is true, Lisa. Did God speak through the prophets of old? Did He as well speak through the Apostles minus one? Do we not have the entire Bible for our benefit and spiritual-growth?" I suggested that Jesus was silent on this subject of homosexuality because he had more pressing and consequential concerns—like our oneness with God, the nature of the kingdom of heaven, our worship of mammon, and our proclivity for hypocrisy. Although it's true that individual verses condemn same-sex relationships, I place my faith in the overarching story of Jesus's radical inclusivity and his willingness to share a meal with anyone, even those judged unworthy or unclean by the standards of the time.

In the same letter, Carey pointed to the Bible of Michael Ryan, a survivalist cult leader and white supremacist from Rulo, Nebraska, who was on death row for the torture and murders of one of his followers and the five-year-old son of yet another follower. Mike had blackened out those parts of the Bible with which he disagreed, which was most of it. Carey hadn't seen Mike's Bible, but his friend, Bob Williams, had and had told him that it was "evil." "Can we truly see God in His light, or is it possible to twist a 'God' by twisting verses according to 'our word' and not 'God's Word'? It's possible, because we are so quickly deceived—and worse, we can deceive others with a word said here & a word whispered there. It's so easy!"

We continued to disagree about the Christian position on and response to homosexuality and didn't discuss it again. Perhaps we each saw the other as blackening and twisting Scripture into what we wanted it to say. But I regret not revisiting this subject years later to see if his position had changed.

Carey claimed that it was easier to be a Christian in prison than it was beyond its walls. His need for God's presence and provision was immense, and he was always mindful of it. To stray from it was perilous: "I have counted on God for so many, many things over the years," he wrote (September 16, 2002). Though I've had fears, stresses, and sorrows, I've known far more sweet moments. I don't always crave God's guidance and companionship and feel too easily that I can go it alone, but in harder times Carey's ability to find God's tender mercies in any situation coaxed (and sometimes provoked) me to do the same. In 2007, when I was trying to make the various moves that God had told me to make, I confessed to Carey in a letter "that my faith falters a bit in the middle of the night & I do get scared." He answered:

> There's a whole lot of newness & change & insecurity that is testing your heart; but, Lisa, my friend, remember and be assured that most esp. at night when demons find you somewhat weak & unguarded & your weapons of the Spirit of God is lay [sic] aside, KNOW that it is then that God flies to your side to keep you safe and sheltered in His mighty hand, in the wings of a Dove! Oh, yes! ☺ Remember and know ... Don't fret, even in the shadows (August 11, 2007).

Carey's stories about his utter dependence on God often uplifted me and spurred me on, but they could also make me feel queasy, edgy. When I read about Carey's experiences with God, I sometimes felt even further away from being the surrendered Christian that I wanted to be and so, a failure. Some part of me was still so hungry for worldly success, power, and approval and the identity that I gained through the pursuit of those ends that I wasn't yet ready to come to the end of myself and be wholly God's. Sometimes, Carey's total saturation in Christianity sickened me like any other pleasure if I partook far too much of it—homemade bread, sleep, sex, nostalgia, or too many episodes of BBC mysteries. Consequently, when a letter arrived from Carey, I sometimes let it sit on the counter for a few hours, even a few days, before I opened it. I knew that what was within would both comfort and goad me.

The greatest witness to Carey's faith in God's promises was how he faced each execution date. If he doubted what awaited him after death, he never shared that with me. "I'm praying and pleading with Him to hold open the door so I can come Home to Him," he wrote (March 28, 2007). Through these times of waiting, he heard God's voice clearly:

> Before I received the date . . . more & more over the years I would feel God's gentle tug at my heart steering me in the right direction to take (and of course He would watch me either take the right direction or take the wrong path); more & more often over the years of course I'd be choosing to heed God's voice and do the right thing [. . .]. Sometimes, in a natural (even Christ-like state of mind & heart) process, I wonder if I'm ready, and the answer is yes! Of course I am [. . .]. Lisa, now I feel that tug MORE, as if God says, 'May 8th! I'm coming for you—to take you Home to be with ME!' [. . .]
>
> Of course there's nothing scary or crazy about His voice as each letter and word is said & felt with so much love & peace . . . Really! This is always present, even more so than before the date, even more so each day; even, when I wake up in the middle of the night, my first thought is of Him and/or the date . . . I'm not really afraid, or scared—this is what I've want[ed] for so long; oh, Lisa! Quite often after Christian visits, I'm feeling so good and moved that I wish I could walk straight to the Chair (and literally & realistically) be present with our Lord Jesus! (April 18, 2007)

Only once that I know of did Carey fall away from his daily Bible study. When he learned on May 2, 2007, that his execution, which had been scheduled for May 8, had been stayed, the news was so devastating that he almost collapsed. He'd hoped that soon, he'd be with God in heaven; instead, he'd been returned to the despair and misery of life on death row. His disappointment was so profound that his hunger for Scripture left him for well over a year, though he continued participating in group Bible studies. "Ever since my May '07 stay of execution, I haven't read the Bible on a regular or daily basis, and sometimes I try my best but in the end drift away and coming back to reading it on a daily event is less than ever; please pray about this for me!" (November 1, 2008). He did eventually get his appetite back, but it wasn't until he'd endured a long, desolate stretch. After that, Carey spent those long, uncertain weeks and days before (and after) each scheduled execution praying to, and hearing from, the God who creates and satisfies our hungers, the God who whispers and shouts, the God who shelters us in his mighty hand.

# 6

## "A Part of Me Wants to Live but Most of Me Does Not"

For the first thirteen years of our friendship, Carey wrestled with the decision of whether to stop, restart, or continue his legal appeals. It was early in 1996 when he first mentioned to me that he wanted to stop fighting and go willingly to his execution:

> On & off since my first day on death row (June 20, 1980), I've been thinking about giving up on my appeals. Over the last year, I've shared this a lot with Dave . . . In the last month, I've written letters [about this] to you and a few others that I write to. I'm tired, Lisa. [. . .] I suppose I just don't want to fight any longer. A part of me wants to live but most of me does not; I want to be finished with things (life). At last. (March 16, 1996)

I don't have any record of my response. Because Carey and I had known each other for less than a year at that point, I wasn't yet aware of just how seriously he meant this. And at that point, it had never occurred to me that a person might want to hasten his or her execution.

Carey had eight scheduled executions: September 20, 1980; August 20, 1982; December 4, 1984; May 9, 1997; January 19, 2000; May 8, 2007; June 14, 2011; and finally, August 14, 2018. I knew him for five; he would ask me to witness the eighth. For at least the last decade of his life, and at various points before then, he was a "volunteer" for execution. According to the Death Penalty Information Organization, a volunteer "[waives] at least part of their ordinary appeals or [terminates] proceedings that would have entitled them to additional [legal] process prior to their execution." When he did fight, almost always at the request of others, he did so reluctantly, half-heartedly.

Though Carey didn't have an execution scheduled in 2003, the matter of whether to drop or continue his appeals was particularly consuming, and we discussed it frequently. It was during this time that I came to understand how frustrating and anguishing it was for him to have to face prolonged appeals, execution dates, and stays of execution. Then, I understood why he wanted to stop fighting the fulfillment of his death sentence. "Legally speaking, I don't think there will be a 'next strategy,'" he wrote on February 14. Alan Peterson, his primary attorney, wanted to file an appeal with the United States Supreme Court (USSC) and continue an appeal in the district court. When Peterson visited Tecumseh on February 11, Carey gave him a letter "legally advising him" not to appeal the death sentence. Then, he fired his district court attorney, Jerry Soucie. He knew that there was a "slim possibility that both Courts may rule in favor of me getting off Death Row" but added that that possibility "really doesn't matter to me. Very soon there will be no turning back in my decisions."

The point at issue was a 2002 decision made by a three-judge panel of the Eighth Circuit Court of Appeals, which stated that Nebraska hadn't sufficiently narrowed the meaning of "exceptional depravity," the aggravating factor by which Carey had been sentenced to death. The state appealed for a rehearing by the full Eighth Circuit Court; and in 2003, seven judges voted to uphold Carey's death sentence, while six dissented. The dissenting judges argued that because he hadn't been given "prior notice of the law to be used against him," namely, that the age of his victims would become part of the exceptional depravity formula by which he'd be sentenced to death, he had been denied his due process. Four of the dissenting judges added that neither the state legislature nor the Nebraska Supreme Court (NSC) had devised a scheme that provided the sentencing body with "a cogent, meaningful basis" for distinguishing which few cases merited a death penalty from the many that didn't.

Carey summarized Peterson's assessment of the situation for me. If the Eighth Circuit Court of Appeals had ruled decisively against him, there would have been no point in appealing to the USSC, as those judges almost always upheld the Eighth Circuit Court's decisions in death penalty cases. But because that court had ruled against Carey in a narrow vote of 7–6, there was at least a chance that the nation's highest court might reverse that ruling. But that wasn't what Carey wanted:

> I am tired and fed up, even with all the strength that our Lord provides each & every day to us. We will see IF the Courts will allow me to voluntarily stop my Death Penalty appeals. [. . .] So far, I haven't shared this Death Penalty news with anyone in my family, which if Dave will come in on Sunday to see me, then I might; however, before I tell my family, I actually want to wait to see what the Courts will do in regards to me dropping everything; I don't want to scare or panic anyone about this (February 4, 2003).

He vowed that if the court allowed him to stop his appeals, he would not grant any interviews with the media, though he said that I was free to talk to reporters.

In early February, one of Carey's sisters died from brain cancer, and this loss put him in a new psychic space. "In some strange way that [he wasn't] certain about," her death influenced his decision to stop appealing. "Physically speaking, I am around these other guys," he wrote on February 22, "but spiritually-mentally-emotionally speaking, I am gearing up for the possibility that I may have to walk to the chair; I can feel the beginning of this process. A seriousness, if I can put it that way; I became conscious of this maybe 4–5 days ago. My mind is made up, if the Courts will let me, Lisa."

Carey was adamant about not fighting his execution; and then, he wasn't. On April 11, 2003, he explained how the reversal came about:

> God impressed upon my heart NOT to stop my appeals. How? I was praying to God that if the 8th Circuit Ct rules against me, I would then stop my appeals—UNLESS He would show me beyond a doubt that He wanted me to live . . . However, He must show me somehow, and in a BIG way! Guess what our Father did. One of my volunteer attorney's, Larry Myers & his secretary ["Rose"] visited me on the 8th (Tuesday), and during that visit, well, they cried, pleading with me to live, and continue my appeals; I've had people ask me in an extreme serious way not to stop my appeals (and hopefully I was not cold hearted since I would not consent to continue my appeals), but this was different—I was praying (and listening) to God as they were making their appeal to me . . . It is a rare jewel when an attorney cries (usually it's the client who is crying).

When Larry and Rose returned, they brought several letters from people urging Carey to continue fighting. That evening, he sat down to compose a letter to Larry and Rose, intending to explain that he hadn't changed his mind; instead, he wrote that he would resume his appeals. He was shocked when he saw what he'd written—or rather, what he believed that God had led him to write. When Larry and Rose visited again the next morning, Carey gave them the letter. "They cried even more than the day before and we all hugged each other. Isn't that something?!?!?! Glory be to God!" Carey signed the forms that would retain Alan Peterson as his attorney and allow him to take the case to the USSC. Thirteen days later, he wrote that "Dave & Donny were both very relieved, of course, that I had changed my mind, and with God's encouragement, I am trying not to look back in regret (or else I might be turned into a pillar of salt!)" (April 11, 2003).

I didn't want to ask my friend how he had come to change his mind about something as consequential as whether he should live or die. I feared that if we discussed this, he might change his mind again. But I was curious. If Carey felt that volunteering for execution was no longer the right choice, what had changed? Had his resolve weakened, causing him to say that it was God who told him to appeal rather than admit it? No, that didn't fit with the man that I knew. Had Carey not heard God correctly? That explanation didn't seem likely either. Had Carey felt that God had initially supported his choice to volunteer and then he didn't? In other words, had God changed his mind? Perhaps.

Carey did look back on this appeal with regret. He had agreed to fight his execution, which had pleased and comforted those family and friends who had urged him to; but he had no desire to continue living on death row. It was a fight he hoped to lose. When Carey learned on June 25—several months earlier than anyone had expected—that the Supreme Court wouldn't be hearing his arguments, he rejoiced. He could have appealed the Court's decision using *Ring v. Arizona* (2002), in which the USSC ruled that according to the Sixth Amendment, a defendant has the right to have a jury, not a judge, decide on the presence of an aggravating factor that qualifies the defendant for the death penalty. In Nebraska, a judge made that decision. But on July 28, Carey wrote that he was done fighting. He would not be appealing under *Ring v. Arizona*, and he was awaiting the announcement of a new execution date.

When Carey faced execution dates, his responses followed a predictable pattern: he followed the legal processes; sometimes he was persuaded to restart or continue his appeals by pressure from an attorney, the needs of a loved one, or the voice of God; sometimes, he stood firm. Either way, he wanted and he didn't want to die. Sometimes Carey felt relief after a stay was issued, but it didn't last. He often expressed dismay and irritation about the family, friends, activists, state senators, and others who came to the prison to try to persuade him to continue his appeals. While waiting for the court to set the date of his 1997 execution, he wrote, "You know what, Lisa? It kind of bugs me when anyone (even if my family should try this as well) wants to see me to try to dissuade me; I mean, I've been here since June, 1980, and there is no reason to come now" (August 2, 1996). And as always, he worried about Dave. In fact, Carey had fought his 1997 execution because he felt that Dave needed him so much that Carey couldn't, in good conscience, leave him. But two years later he wrote that instead of fighting so that he could remain here for Dave, he was now focused on "trying to help Dave (and myself as well thank God) be prepared for my death, for our separation from each other" (October 2, 1999).

His preparations included the practical and the emotional. In 2007, he removed his name and address from junk mail lists. He made a will and arranged for his possessions to be distributed among those who needed them. He found people who could pay for his cremation. He gave prison officials a list of the people that he was willing to visit during the week before his execution, and he chose his personal spiritual advisor and the other three people who would witness his execution. He tried to be "optimistic & positive" and to keep his emotions from "flying all over the place" (April 20, 2007). The closer he came to the date of execution, the "more ready" he was to be with God; and in the weeks prior to one such date, the stress headaches from which he'd been suffering suddenly stopped. Despite wanting to be executed, he was afraid. "Yes, it will most definitely be hard to walk straight to the Chair but, on the other hand, it won't be that hard with Jesus holding on to my hand every step of the way. Glory be to God!!!! ☺)" (March 5, 2007).

Part of Carey's preparations for his 2007 execution involved a medical negligence lawsuit that he was planning to file against the state involving a torn anterior cruciate ligament in his left knee. For several years, he'd sought help with the pain that resulted when one of the two pins that the surgeon had placed in his knee had come partway out. And from February 2005 to January 2007, he'd left a paper trail documenting his unsuccessful efforts to get the medical care he needed.

Carey needed someone to represent his estate in the lawsuit if he was executed. "I need a person to act on my behalf until this case is settled or dropped, which if I win will force new rules and regulations, thus forcing prison medical to take care of Death Row inmates much better than they have in the past" (April 13, 2007). Five days later he wrote, "Well, if this was Valentine's Day, try to finish this sentence . . . 'Will you be my____?' Well, this is just a little humor. ☺ Seriously though, will you be my . . . 'personal representative'?" I spoke by telephone with Carey and one of his attorneys, Edward Fogarty, about this matter. I was honored that they trusted me to handle it, and I agreed to be the representative. But I was also shaken by Carey's matter-of-fact approach to his death; and in the back of my mind, I began to fear that *his* prayer requests would be fulfilled, after all.

A few days later, I received a thick envelope from Fogarty containing "documents tracing the two years of inattention to Mr. Moore's left knee problem [2/6/05–1/26/07]," including notes about a doctor who he named, who'd joked that an execution would solve Carey's knee problem. Without a doubt, he had been, as Carey had written earlier, "the wrong Dr. for the job." Carey's will stated that if damages were to be paid, he wanted 50 percent to go to NADP and 50 percent to "the children living at the time of my death of Reuel Eugene Van Ness, Jr., and Maynard D. Helgeland." Any money that their heirs refused would also go to NADP. He bequeathed his television set to Raymond Mata, his typewriter to Arthur Gales, his footlocker to Jeffrey Hessler, and anything else—his poetry, books, papers, money left on his account, if there was any—to Dave.

Carey was relieved that I had agreed to be his legal representative and that his attorneys, Fogarty, Myers, and Peterson, had offered to help Dave pay for the cremation and memorial service. "Bless their heart! This takes a BIG load off my mind, praise God!" Then he added, "It was good speaking to you on the phone last night, and I like hearing you laugh—I always have! I think I've said that before to you, so it must be true! ☺" (April 21, 2007). Unfortunately, nothing came of his preparations: Carey didn't file the lawsuit, and his left knee was never fixed.

As Carey prepared for executions, I was in an uncomfortable position. As much as I respected my friend's right to self-determination, I didn't want to lose him or see his death be used for anyone's political and financial gain. It felt wrong for me not to try to change the situation; after all, I had been acquainted with three death row inmates who were resentenced to life in prison and knew of one death row inmate who had been released in 2001 after the charges against him were dropped. There was at least a chance that Carey's circumstances might change if someone could persuade him to restart his appeals. And yet, I couldn't ask him to endure under conditions that were destructive to his body, mind, and spirit. Nor could I argue with his desire to die—or more accurately, not to go on living—in order to be free of the sorrow, brutality, and hopelessness of prison life and fulfill his yearning to be finally and completely with God. So, I learned to live with these contrary impulses and ultimately came to see his decision to not fight his execution as a rational one, given the extreme circumstances in which he lived.

My responses to Carey's execution dates also followed a predictable pattern. Many times a day from the moment I first heard about an execution date until it was stayed, I was aware of something awful looming. I couldn't stop myself from imagining the circumstances of my friend's violent, public, and politicized end. I imagined him wanting to escape execution and life in a maximum-security prison but everywhere he turned, he faced a cement wall or a locked steel door—my own nightmare. With his permission, I'd do whatever I could to convince state officials to change their minds about carrying out his sentence, which meant writing letters to various officials and holding signs at vigils and protests. I also offered to speak on his behalf at a commutation hearing. "I'll tell them that I'd feel safe leaving my kids in your care," I told him. But his answer was always the same: Thank you, but there will be no commutation hearing. Otherwise, I should do what I needed to do. But, he added, if I prayed for a stay, I shouldn't "pray too hard." In the end, there was nothing for me to do but tell him that I supported his choice—even as I sometimes worked against his desires. When I prayed, I didn't ask for a legal win that would release my friend from execution or death row. Instead, I told God that I didn't know what to ask for other than wisdom, peace, and healing for all of us involved.

When an execution was looming, I wrote to Carey more often than usual to show my support for him. At such times, I told him how much I valued his friendship and that I didn't want to be without him—a selfish but heartfelt sentiment. For the most part, I avoided discussions of whether or not I thought that he should fight his execution; yet, on a few occasions, I couldn't resist telling him that I feared that if he went willingly to his execution, it would make easier for the state to kill others on death row. He said that he'd heard that argument from many people. "If anything, it may help others if the electrocution goes wrong." He insisted that that didn't make him "some sort of a martyr" (April 18, 2007). I found no comfort or value in him suffering such an agonizing death, even if it was for the sake of others.

Mostly, Carey and I wrote about the ordinary details of our lives. Although I was glad to distract him with news of my mother's neck surgery, Ian's new job, Meredith's science fair project, or my crashed computer, it felt trite and insensitive for me to fret, grieve, or rejoice over such matters when he was facing death. But he responded to my stories with warmth and interest, and he wrote to me about the details of his life: a visit from his brother John and sister-in-law Glory ("praise God!!!"); his thoughts on Miriam and Aaron's jealousy toward their brother, Moses, and the favor God showed him; a rumor that death row was being moved to the hole; the problem with people who value one spiritual gift—like speaking in tongues—over the others; his gratitude for the people in his life: "I am so thankful that

I have caring friends on my side; Lisa, I thank you sincerely, my friend!" (November 3, 2003).

I wasn't the only one writing to him: in the times just before his execution dates, Carey received far more letters than usual. "I am writing much shorter letters—they're exhausting and I just can't handle it! ☺" (March 31, 2007). Unfortunately, some letters that he received were angry and critical. Some of these came from people he knew; others came from strangers. "Their attitudes are very upsetting. No, I did not expect them to be approv[ing] of my actions but, well, some are very disappointing of me and very angry" (March 28, 2007). Some letter writers said that they could no longer be friends with him if he volunteered for execution. One nationally known death penalty abolitionist, author, and professor with whom Carey had corresponded for several years wrote "a real awful letter about my decision. [. . .] This surprised me" (March 28, 2007). While I regretted that Carey had to deal with such responses, I understood what motivated them. Like me, these correspondents did not want to lose a friend. Like me, what they were *really* angry about was the existence of the death penalty.

But some people touched him with their concern. State Senator Dwite Pedersen came to TSCI to persuade Carey to fight his execution. Carey wrote to me of his respect for and enjoyment of Pedersen. About the same time, State Senator Ernie Chambers wrote Carey "an incredible, thoughtful, and heartfelt letter." But neither senator could convince him to resume his appeals.

And so, we waited. When I opened the newspaper or turned on the news, I did so with hope and fear. "I haven't heard a peep from the Courts or from the A.G.'s office, in regard to a possible execution date," Carey wrote. "I'm waiting to hear something, even anything is the difficult part for me" (February 21, 2007). How anxiety-provoking it must have been to have to look in the morning newspaper for updates on when and how he was going to be killed. I hadn't seen or heard signs of depression in Carey during our visits and phone calls, or even in his letters. But I didn't know what he was experiencing when alone in his cell. When I asked him if he was depressed, he answered, "maybe some," but that wasn't a factor in his decision not to fight his execution. On one occasion, he had contact with a mental health professional, but I don't know what that entailed.

On February 27, 2007, Attorney General Jon Bruning requested that the NSC set Carey's execution for May 8. Carey refused to file a state or federal appeal which might have stopped or delayed it. "I am simply tired and worn out from being on death row all the years, and I don't want to wait for another possible year to get off [. . .]. I am praying and pleading with God to open the door so I can come Home to Him . . . it's as simple as that I guess." Sometimes he surprised me with his jokes. "If I actually get a date, I know I won't believe it until maybe 24 hours after the execution" (March 10, 2007). And sometimes he surprised me with his bluntness: death had been fast for his victims but was slow for him.

In the early years of the millennium, Carey had been typing most of his letters to me. But he was so confident that this execution would be carried out that he saw no reason to invest in new typing supplies. "I am writing to everyone by hand, as I am out of ribbon to type with; but, that's okay—another month to go hopefully and Lord willing" (March 28, 2007). His philosophical statements about being ready for death no longer surprised me. But I was still rattled by his calm, clear-headed attention to the details of leaving this life, like when he filed a humanitarian motion requesting that he be executed a day earlier than scheduled, since the birthday of fellow death row inmate Jose Sandoval fell on May 8 "and I don't want his every birthday to be remembered with my execution." His request was denied.

While the State of Nebraska had killed three men in the electric chair during the 1990s, I'd seen many more execution dates, both for Carey and others, come and go. So, I believed it was more likely than not that his 2007 execution would be stayed, too. On May 2, I rejoiced at the news that because the NDCS had failed to follow a state law requiring public hearings and state oversight when devising the new execution protocol, Senator Chambers requested that this protocol be reviewed before anyone else was put to death. NSC Judge John Gerrard, writing for the four to three majority, said that recent USSC decisions, as well as appeals from Nebraska death row inmate Raymond Mata Jr., presented the court with the question of whether electrocution is consistent with the prohibitions in the US and Nebraska constitutions on cruel and unusual punishment. Because Mata's appeal was still pending, the NSC had acted prematurely when it issued a death warrant for Carey and so, his execution was stayed.

Carey was devastated about being yanked back from the edge. "My knees almost buckled beneath me and I almost collapsed to the floor. I was in shock! No way!" (June 6, 2018). As happy as I was, I felt deeply for him. I could imagine how difficult it would be to return to a job that I'd quit, a house that I'd vacated, or a man that I'd left. But I couldn't imagine what it must have been like to have to return to one's former prison cell when one was a mere six days away from permanent release. I did, however, find some parallels to my father's almost decade-long battle with cancer. When I'd received the news that he'd been diagnosed with intermediate-stage prostate cancer, I felt that I had to prepare myself for his death, which then I thought would come sooner than later. But shortly afterward, my dad began to participate in experimental treatments at Cleveland Clinic that, though physically grueling, gave him hope and seemed to have bought him time. As the years passed, we believed his cancer was less threatening. Perhaps he could—*had*—beaten it. I'd go days, weeks, even, without thinking about it. But then, he became too sick to continue with the clinical trials. After the long reprieve, I once again had to face the fact that my father had a disease that would probably kill him. He died not long after. In 2018, Carey explained that as the 2007 execution neared, he'd had "both feet in the 'ready to meet the Lord' gear," but he'd been forced to change his thinking when he'd learned that he wouldn't be going "Home." I wondered why, at times like these, he didn't consider taking his own life. Maybe he did; but he never told me, and I never asked, for fear that he might think that I was suggesting such an action.

As he faced his final execution date in 2018, Carey wrote that he had to protect himself by putting his thinking "half in gear or half full charge ahead [. . .] so my heart wouldn't be so twisted up inside should God decide to give me a Stay again because let's face it, 'anything' is possible" (July 6, 2018). This quote reveals that Carey saw not the court, an attorney, or an appeal as responsible for his stays of execution, but God. Though he didn't always agree with or understand God's decision, he was sure that God knew what he was doing and that it was his job to accept it. Following his stayed execution in 2007, he wrote:

> Lisa, my friend, I really am tired, but "God" must surely have a most wonderful plan for me and for ALL of us; He is the One who stopped my execution date. I was there at NSP [in the hospital on death watch] for almost three days, and my mind & heart was firmly on the door that opened unto Jesus . . . but, well, I won't cry over spilled milk, or complain about it. God's ways are so much higher than ours, praise God!!! ☺ Last night at supper, I began to feel like my old self again; please continue to help me, Lord (May 9, 2007).

Following the 2007 stay, Peterson, a fellow Christian, asked Carey for one last chance to represent him in the Eighth Circuit Court of Appeals. Just months before he was executed, Carey looked back on this time: "I wasn't going to consent but he politely twisted my arm by saying that 'I owe him' for all the years he has volunteered his services to all the court appointed attorney's (since he was my attorney in 1987), and I couldn't say no to him (at that time) as I watched his earnestness. I consented" (May 31, 2018). Carey doubted that the appeal would be successful. On May 24 he wrote that if the court ruled against Raymond Mata's claim that the electric chair was cruel and unusual punishment, "thus saying something like one long 20 second current is not cruel & unusual punishment, well, it would be worthless for me to appeal any longer." Even so, he now regretted giving in to Peterson's request.

After his return to death row at the Tecumseh prison on May 3, he tackled the thirty to forty letters that awaited him, including one from me. He was also concerned about recovering or replacing his TV set, radio, CD player, and typewriter, which had helped fill the long, idle hours with distraction and sustaining routines. "Now I suppose I have to start from the ground up—just like a new guy would" (May 9, 2007). With contributions from Dave Moore and Alan Peterson totaling $266, he was able to buy back his television and typewriter. Yet he still needed $47.97 for a CD player and $37.97 for a clock radio, plus ribbons and correctable tape. On May 27, he thanked me for my contribution and told me that George Eisele had helped, too.

In spite of Carey's belief that God's response to "prayer by many" had prevented him from going to his death, he wasn't at peace, nor was he his old self. June 20, 2007, was the twenty-seventh anniversary of his arrival on death row, an anniversary that he had hoped he wouldn't live to see. I asked him if he regretted how things had turned out. He answered:

> Yes, "I feel" I have changed from what or due to what I'd went through [...]. And just like a "Cancer Survivor," there's change—whether bad or good; sometimes, sometimes mind you, I feel maybe the change was for the bad. But I am still praying. ☺ Yes, beyond a doubt, I "regret how things turned out" . . . I feel like a part of me is still at NSP in that room in the hospital ward being watched by two prison staff 24 hours a day, and I won't be whole (one person) until they take this body back (June 20, 2007).

Because Carey believed that God had stayed the 2007 execution, he promised to continue appealing, even though he didn't want to. "Yes, I have decided to appeal again," he wrote on January 12, 2009. "God decided this decision when he gave me a Stay back in May '07, so I need not wrestle with that argument within myself." He would refer to this 2007 decision as "my promise," and he saw it as a turning point.

But in 2011, when facing yet another execution date, he broke his promise. "I don't want to pursue this subject in the Courts, even if it will get me off death row. I am simply tired of this," he wrote on July 7, 2011. He wanted to keep his word to both God and his attorneys that he would allow them to represent him in court, but he felt that "five years since 'my promise'" was enough. Consequently, in early December, Carey filed motions in Douglas County District Court asking the judge "not to accept any motions from my attorney, Jerry Soucie" (December 21, 2011). He sent copies of his request to the attorney general and Soucie.

I asked Carey if he'd broken his promise to God or if God had released him from it when he stopped his appeals. He didn't directly answer my question but wrote that his situation reminded him of that of Abraham and Sarah. "The angel or God's messenger told them they would have a child but then they became a bit impatient (especially her) on Him. Time and distance, I'm not sure, Lisa, possibly. I've seen guys get off Death Row, mostly to Life sentences—what ugly futures in my humble opinion" (June 14, 2018).

Was Carey, like Sarah and Abraham, intent on rushing a process rather than waiting on God to fulfill the promise that he'd made in God's own time? Or did he believe that sometimes, God needed a little push in keeping his promises?

Most people sentenced to death in the United States do not want to die. Through extensive state and federal appeals processes, they and their attorneys delay execution by months, years, or even decades. Some die of old age or illness before their appeals are exhausted. And yet, since the death penalty was reinstated in 1976, about 11 percent of those sentenced to death have sought to accelerate that end by dismissing their legal counsel and waiving their constitutional right to have their cases brought before a higher court—just as Carey had done so many times.

To understand what motivates one to volunteer, Meredith Rountree, a law professor at Northwestern University, studied the public statements of two groups of thirty-one "similarly situated death-sentenced prisoners" who were executed in Texas: one group after abandoning their appeals, and the other in spite of their efforts to fight execution. One might assume that the volunteers were mentally ill. But Rountree says that as the majority of people on death row are mentally ill (more so than in the general prison population), "mental illness alone does not clearly distinguish the volunteer from the non-volunteer."

The Texas volunteers that Rountree studied shared several traits. Hopelessness factored strongly in their choice, even though a death sentence *isn't* necessarily hopeless in a legal sense. In Texas, for instance, a state that kills far more of its death-sentenced than any other and where the appeals process has been streamlined, 56 percent of those sentenced to death *aren't* executed, due to successful appeals, natural death, or suicide. What the volunteers couldn't trust was the possibility of creating a tolerable—much less meaningful—life in prison. Winning a life sentence wouldn't lessen their despair. Carey himself feared such a sentence, as it meant living in the general population, which, with its riots, rapes, gangs, and illegal drugs, was a meaner, less protected place than death row. It would also have fewer of the opportunities and resources needed for a successful appeal.

Rountree found that most volunteers shared a cluster of factors: they were more likely than those fighting their sentences to have been previously convicted of a crime, especially one against another person; to have been previously incarcerated; to have committed the murder alone, as acting with another diffuses one's sense of responsibility; and to have done so with a gun. Those who killed their intimate partners were at higher risk for suicide, and those who committed their capital crime during a domestic crisis were "overrepresented in Texas executions." In fact, 25.8 percent of the Texas volunteer population committed an offense related to an intimate partner dispute, while only 7.4 percent of those who fought their executions in Texas had committed such a crime. Apparently, the guilt and stigma that accompanies killing one's spouse or lover contribute to the shame and hopelessness that might convince someone that they deserved to die and should take steps to hasten the fulfillment of their sentence.

Carey fit this profile in several ways. He had spent thirteen months in jail for auto theft. Though he'd involved his brother in what would become a robbery and murder, a decision that he would deeply regret for the rest of his life, he'd committed the second murder alone. For both murders, he'd used a handgun. Most volunteers said that their death sentence was just, which Rountree read as an effort to "normalize to others their desire to die." I never heard Carey say that his sentence was just, and I never heard him say that it wasn't. But then, I never asked.

Prison conditions are another contributing factor. More highly segregated environments lead to higher rates of volunteering because they so erode mental health that death seems preferable to life in isolation. In a 2016 study, the Vera Institute of Justice, an independent nonprofit whose mission is to improve "justice systems," reported that the Nebraska prison system used solitary confinement at twice the national rate. The "hole" that Carey wrote so frequently about was "a jail within the prison" with far fewer privileges than either the general or death row populations. I can imagine why one might find death preferable to such frequent and prolonged isolation. Even for one with Carey's spiritual reserves, time in the hole was harrowing. According to him, it was overused, and the threat of being sent there was ever-present. On one of the occasions when those on death row were placed in solitary confinement, Carey wrote:

> I received your letter very late last night, praise God, and I sure needed the encouragement that you gave me from it!!! My heart was so heavy last night; yesterday was Death Row's very first day in the hole (called SMU or Special Management Unit) [. . .] I spent last night with God (which is not uncommon of course),

but I was more earnest, praise God! There's a beautiful Christian song that gave me so much peace of heart and mind, titled: "Because He Lives" by William ☺ Gaither & Gloria Gather.

I had to repeat the chorus many many times before I felt a release [of] some of the tension & stress I was feeling all day, which was only building up and getting worse. God IS good, Lisa! Thank you for your letter! You inquired why the move? I suspect that this has been their plans even from the beginning for us on Death Row (January 15, 2003).

Most arguments in support of the rights of a man (those sentenced to death are almost always men) to waive his appeals contend that giving him the freedom to choose when he dies enhances his dignity in humiliating and agonizing circumstances. But Rountree argues that this line of reasoning doesn't acknowledge "the difficulty in identifying free action for individuals facing death and immersed in these complicated psychosocial dynamics," such as idleness, isolation, loneliness, and hopelessness, as well as the psychological stress of awaiting one's death by such calculated means. "Death row phenomenon," or the emotional distress that one experiences while living for a long time under the harsh, dehumanizing conditions of death row, can result in "Death Row Syndrome," the symptoms of which, according to psychiatrist Harold I. Schwartz, range from "extreme anxiety, to dissociation, to full-blown psychosis." Certainly, such symptoms would interfere with one's ability to make a sound decision. Unfortunately, some arguments in support of one's right to volunteer for execution overlook or downplay the state's interest in fair and constitutional death sentences, something that requires a complex and thorough appeals process to ensure that the state doesn't execute the wrongly convicted.

To volunteer for execution, an inmate must notify the court that he is dropping his appeals or dismissing legal counsel. The court then decides if the inmate is mentally competent and has made a knowing, voluntary, and intelligent waiver of his rights. But there are problems with such a method of determining mental competency. Since the reinstatement of the death penalty in 1976, about the same number of people have volunteered as have been exonerated. But the two groups are treated very differently. The legal process leading to exoneration is subjected to careful scrutiny, but the cases of those who have sought to circumvent legal procedures designed to make sure that only the "worst of the worst" are executed have received far less attention. Among those who relinquish their right to appeal are those who might have been exonerated or resentenced had their convictions received adversarial scrutiny.

The appellate review process is critical because it ensures that the condemned receive fair treatment and aren't wrongly executed and demonstrates that as a society, we are following our own laws. When an inmate receives inadequate representation or waives his or her appeals, society is denied the fair and complete review of a high-stakes process that can be riddled with errors or influenced by biases. In his dissenting opinion in *Gilmore v. Utah* (1976), in which Gary Gilmore's mother, Bessie, acted as his "next friend" or representative and filed for a stay of her son's execution, Supreme Court Justice Thurgood Marshall wrote that without appellate review, "an unacceptably high percentage of criminal defendants would be wrongfully executed—'wrongfully' because they were innocent of the crime, undeserving of the severest punishment relative to similarly situated offenders, or denied essential procedural protections by the State." In 2021, the Death Penalty Information Center reported that since 1973, more than one hundred eighty people had been released from their death sentences because the evidence proved their innocence. The Center website also provided photos and brief biographical statements of eighteen people who were executed between 1989 and 2019 but were most likely innocent. The delays that result from adversarial testing of the fairness of convictions and sentences are not only justified but necessary if they prevent the wrongly convicted from being executed. But when volunteers waive their rights early in the process, fewer convictions and sentences are scrutinized—and fewer wrong convictions are overturned.

Volunteering may also be used as a permanent solution to a temporary problem. Because the mental health of the volunteer is rarely thoroughly and professionally examined or tested, it's hard to know if the condemned is making an informed and independent decision. But, says John H. Blume of Cornell Law School, it's not only the inmate's mental competency, the current legal standard for volunteering, that needs to be examined but his *motives* as well. Is the condemned choosing to accept a legal outcome? Or is the condemned seeking a state-assisted suicide?

Carey knew that his state of mind influenced his decision to volunteer (or not). "Most (if not all prisoners) feel depressed about being locked up [. . .]," he wrote on May 6, 2004. "I sometimes think that some/many animals in zoos might have these same feelings of depression . . . esp. when people gawk at them and even make faces at them." He didn't want to stop his appeals because he was more depressed than usual about "where I am at and the amount of years, so I tried to be open with the shrink here and the medical dr, and the dr prescribed Prozac." While on the antidepressant, Carey still wanted to die, though he felt "less stress" about being on death row and in prison. But because Prozac created "false feelings" that hindered his ability to deal with "all types of prison situations," he stopped taking it.

Noting the striking similarities between volunteers for execution and people outside of prison who die by suicide, Blume turned to laws about suicide for guidance. In almost every Western democracy and state in the US, it's a crime to assist a suicide, with the single exception of physician-assisted suicide of the terminally ill, which is legal in several states. Blume says that if it weren't for the fact that the inmate had been sentenced to death, it would be illegal in virtually every jurisdiction for anyone to assist an inmate in actively hastening his own death. Moreover, it's irrelevant whether the inmate's choice seems logical or not; just as with suicide, we don't deem it an acceptable solution merely because the person's choice seems rational. "Even persons in extreme pain, persons with no hope of improvement, persons certain to lose their mental abilities, or persons imposing enormous financial or psychological costs on family members can be prevented from committing suicide, and others are prohibited from assisting suicide," Blume says. Volunteering for execution in order "to deliberately terminate one's own life," the definition of suicide, should be considered an assisted suicide and thus, illegal. Blume recommends that the law require a judge to discern whether a potential volunteer "truly accepts the justness of his punishment [if indeed it is just], or whether he was seeking to commit suicide." But either way, the inmate is choosing to go willingly to his death. And would that inmate have reached a different conclusion if he had had access to mental health services and if prisons relied less on solitary confinement?

The night before the new owner gained possession of his house, Ian's father slipped a noose around his neck and jumped from the table that he'd positioned beneath a strong branch of the silver maple tree in his backyard. When my son and I helped resolve Gerald's domestic and financial affairs, we discovered many testaments—the Dollar General receipt in his wallet for the rope with which he'd hanged himself, the fact that he hadn't packed up and vacated his house—to the hopelessness, misery, and regret that had marked his final weeks. Though he and I had parted ways decades earlier, I wondered if there was anything that Ian and I could have said or done to have prevented his death, to have helped him find a reason to hope, to live. As I reread Carey's letters during the spring and summer of 2018, I saw that same awful momentum gathering up his frustration and despair. On May 18, less than three months before his execution, he insisted that he wasn't depressed but exhausted. I can't judge if my friend was depressed, but I can say that he was worn down, worn out, and bereft of hope.

# 7

# Behind the Headlines

For the first six years of our friendship, death row was housed at the Nebraska State Penitentiary in Lincoln, positioned at the corner of Nebraska Highway 2 and South Fourteenth Street. When I drove past, I often saw inmates walking the track or playing ball. Sometimes, I could even see the armed guards watching them in the towers dotting the wall that surrounded most of the yard. And of course, when I saw the parking lot, I remembered the night when my family, friends, and I had participated in a vigil and protest there. For several years, I regularly visited Carey at NSP. Because of my claustrophobia, I was mildly panicky for the few minutes I had to spend in what I called "the holding cage" before a guard buzzed open the door to the visiting area. Otherwise, being locked in was manageable. While I waited for Carey to arrive, I'd stand at the windows and gaze at the coil of razor wire that sat atop a tall chain-link fence and the strip of sky above it, or else look across the street, at Burger King and a cold storage facility that always seemed to be hiring.

This was where Carey lived from ages twenty-two to forty-four. For awhile, he claimed that Nebraska had "one of the best Death Row's in the U.S. and in the world" (February 4, 1998). But change was coming. Several intertwined national trends resulted in US prisons being filled beyond their capacity. Between the 1970s and the 1990s, the so-called "war on drugs" introduced mandatory minimum sentencing for drug-related offenses, resulting in longer incarcerations. The "tough-on-crime" policies of the eighties and nineties culminated in the passage of the Violent Crime Control and Law Enforcement Act of 1994, which included the draconian "three strikes" provision. Under this law, a third felony conviction usually brought a life sentence with no possibility of parole until a considerable amount of time, most commonly twenty-five years, had been served. Because of such laws, the US prison population has, according to the Sentencing Project, grown by 500 percent in the past forty years, to nearly 2.2 million. In 2018, Congress passed and President Trump signed the First Step Act, which took modest steps at sentencing reform by shortening mandatory sentences for federal prisoners who'd committed nonviolent drug offenses. Unfortunately, this doesn't affect most of the 2.12 million people in prison, as only 152,464 of them are in federal facilities as of 2020.

The growth in the US prison population is illogical. Violent crime has declined since the mid-1980s, yet the number of life sentences has more than quadrupled since then. (In contrast, the number of death sentences imposed has fallen from 315 in 1996 to thirty-four in 2019, according to the Death Penalty Information Center.) But rather than reducing prison sentences, state legislatures are more likely to authorize funding for new prisons and cut spending for what actually reduces crime—mental health services, educational enrichment programs for at-risk populations, and a strong social safety net—in the process. According to a 2020 report from the Open Sky Policy Institute, a nonpartisan think tank that focuses its research and analysis on tax and budget issues, the Nebraska legislature's biennial budget reports dating back to the fiscal year 1997 reveal that general fund appropriations to the Department of Education increased by an annual average of 3.77 percent. During that same period, however, appropriations to the Department of Corrections grew by an average of 6.08 percent per year. Likewise, growth in appropriations for all fund sources averaged 3.82 percent for K–12 education and 5.95 percent annually for Corrections.

The prison-building boom fueled—and in turn, was fueled by—the growth of what some call the "prison-industrial complex" (PIC), a combination of private and government interests that collectively profit from incarceration and increased spending on prisons, whether it is warranted or not. In the December 1998 issue of *The Atlantic*, investigative journalist Eric Schlosser says that rather than a conspiracy secretly guiding the nation's criminal justice policy, the PIC is "composed of politicians, both liberal and conservative, who have used the fear of crime to gain votes; impoverished rural areas where prisons have become a cornerstone of economic development; private companies that regard the roughly $35 billion spent each year on corrections not as a burden on American taxpayers but as a lucrative market for the companies; and government officials whose fiefdoms have expanded along with the inmate population." (Schlosser was writing in 1998. According to more recent Bureau of Justice statistics, the United

States now spends about $80 billion annually on corrections, though in 2017, the Equal Justice Initiative put the figure at $182 billion.) As a result of these powerful interests, the United States, which has about 5 percent of the global population but 25 percent of the world's prisoners, now has the highest incarceration rate in the world, and prison construction has, according to Schlosser, "a seemingly unstoppable momentum."

This momentum is evident in Nebraska which has, as Henry J. Cordes reports in the January 9, 2022 *Omaha World-Herald*, the fastest growing inmate population in the country. In December 2020, Scott Frakes, the director of the NDCS, asked for $230 million to build a new, 1,512-bed prison to ease overcrowding. Appropriations Committee chairperson John Stinner estimated that the new prison would require an additional 434 million per year in operating costs. On April 20, 2021, Grant Schulte reported that in spite of objections from some state senators that money would be better spent on education, housing, mental health, and other services, the unicameral approved funding for the planning and design of the new prison and set aside $115 million to cover half of the total cost of the project even though it hadn't yet been approved. In 2022, Frakes was scouting for a building site, even though the new prison, which had the support of Governor Ricketts, still hadn't been approved by the legislature.

Problems such as poverty, mental illness, drug and alcohol addiction, and lack of education are easier to ignore when many of those most profoundly affected by them are hidden behind concrete walls and razor wire. Of course, people who have committed serious crimes *should* serve just sentences. But to expect functioning, much less favorable outcomes, from an institution that is overcrowded, understaffed, and too reliant on solitary confinement or that fails to adequately prepare the incarcerated for a meaningful life beyond or within the prison or that is structured so that the powerful can profit from the misfortunes of others, is irrational. So, too, it is irrational to expect people who have been incarcerated in such places to make a successful re-entry into society upon their release.

In 1997, when the Nebraska unicameral authorized the building of a new medium- and maximum-security prison to ease overcrowding, it was part of a national trend in which state governments saw high-security prisons as the way to reduce prison risk and violence while being easier to manage and fund than traditional prisons like NSP. In the January 18, 2011, issue of the *New Humanist*, Sharon Shalev, a criminologist and expert on the use of solitary confinement, writes that the bunker-like supermax prisons that popped up across the United States in the 1990s were seen as management tools that would effectively isolate risk and control violence because they were "calculated to design out human contact and enable maximum prisoner isolation and control." Because they relied on single-cell confinement and enhanced security technology, supermax prisons cost two or three times as much to build and operate as traditional prisons. Various studies show that it costs about three times as much to house an inmate in a Special Management Unit cell as it does a non-SMU cell.

When I was a child, people fought to keep prisons out of their communities. But that has changed in the past several decades. Many of those in small towns that had suffered population and economic losses because of the shift from a manufacturing to a service economy, from family to corporate farming, and from local businesses to chain stores hoped and believed that a prison would provide secure jobs and customers for their motels, restaurants, and convenience shops as long as there was a steady supply of inmates from the urban parts of the state, which the long sentences handed down under the tough-on-crime laws and the war on drugs would provide. In fact, as Tracy Huling writes in "Building A Prison in Rural America," prisons have become "one of the three leading rural economic enterprises" (the other two are casinos and huge animal confinement units) "as states and localities seek industries which provide large scale and quick opportunities." When I lived in southern Illinois during the mid-1990s, I watched with wonder as a nearby town with about 3,800 residents, once home to a coal company, offered $8 million and free land as incentives to entice the state to locate a new correctional center there. When the townspeople received news that they had "won" the medium-security prison, they closed the schools for the day, rang the church bells, and celebrated. Numerous towns in Nebraska put in bids to host the new medium- and maximum-security prison in the late 1990s. The top two contenders were Tecumseh, in the far southeastern corner of the state, and McCook, in the far southwestern corner. One of the reasons that Tecumseh was chosen over McCook was because of its higher unemployment rate. Surely, a new prison would fix that and give the residents cause for celebration.

But prisons aren't the boon that people expect. The highest-paying jobs rarely go to locals. Many employees choose not to live in the same town as the prison. In the case of the Tecumseh State Correctional Institution, the town of Tecumseh, with a population of 1,586 in 2019, can't offer the amenities or provide the workforce that Lincoln or the Omaha-Council Bluffs metropolitan areas (populations of about 289,000 and 1,058,000, respectively, in 2019), or even Beatrice (population 12,300) can, which means that the prison employees who live in those cities don't own property, shop, pay taxes, or participate in community events in the town where they work, though they might buy gas, coffee, and snacks there. And greater tax revenue is what towns and counties that host prisons need, as their budgets for legal and medical services and infrastructure are often burdened by the demands of a prison.

In May 1998, then-DCS director Harold Clarke announced that the new, $74 million medium- and maximum-security prison that would house 960 inmates and employ about 430 people with an annual payroll of $13.7 million, had been awarded to Tecumseh, fifty-five miles from Lincoln and seventy-seven miles from Omaha, the two cities where the families of most inmates lived. Though death row would be located in the Tecumseh facility, executions would still take place at the prison in Lincoln. Steve King, the NDCS's planning and research manager, stated that when the prison opened, the Nebraska correctional system would be at 120 percent capacity—still overcrowded. And according to then-state ombudsman Marshall Lux, from the start, there was concern whether a prison in this location could attract enough employees.

Carey saw the new high-security prison as a grave misuse of tax dollars. "I think it's real stupid that Nebraska is paying to have a Super-maximum prison built. Very stupid," he wrote on June 20, 1998. "Instead, they should increase the buildings and esp. the staff in this prison; a lot of money would be saved!" His plan was sounder than that of state officials, as it was frugal and would have created safer conditions for both staff and inmates. Apparently, those aren't the priorities of the prison-industrial complex.

What Carey and others on death row learned about their new residence through newspaper articles, prison communications, and rumors worried them. He was particularly concerned about a prison memorandum he'd heard about that said that inmates in administrative segregation would have tele-visits, though the general population would continue to have "contact" visits. He didn't know if those on death row would have the same rules as those in administrative segregation or the general population (May 11, 2001). Certainly, inmates and families found contact visits more satisfying than tele-visits. Various studies, including one done by the Minnesota Department of Corrections in 2011, show a link between regular contact visits and both better behavior while in prison and a decrease in criminal behavior after release. It's healing and motivating to hold one's child or hug one's spouse, parent, or sibling and look them in the face while having a conversation. But most media coverage of the new prison was focused on the physical facilities and said little about such conditions and their consequences.

After months of delay, death row moved to Tecumseh in May 2002.

> I won't say (yet) if the stress here is either less, or the same, or even more but I hear that there are MANY in TSCI population

> who says that life is so much worse than NSP; I think I believe that. Beyond a doubt, Death Row yard is WORSE here than NSP, and a lot smaller; yard here is a small area, 3 tall brick walls with a tall fence (as a fourth wall) that has barb & razor wire strung on top of it. There is no table(s) or chair(s), nothing to sit on only there's one baskball [sic] & one basketball hoop. That is it. The visiting room is larger than NSP and ceilings taller (picture a gymnasium without bleachers.) Visitors are pat-searched coming in and every time they use the restroom; including children; Dave's daughter Taylor, who is only 5 yrs. old, was pat-searched after using the restroom, as was Dave (May 27, 2002).

The new prison presented challenges for me, as well. Even though Carey was strong and resilient, I worried about how the harsher conditions might affect him. He would be confined to a "dog kennel" for outdoor recreation and have fewer visitors and Bible studies. I knew that I would see him less often: a round-trip drive from my home in northwest Lincoln, across the city, and to Tecumseh required two and a half to three hours, depending on the traffic. At that time, I was commuting to the university in Omaha two or three times a week during the fall and spring semesters and was reluctant to add yet another drive. And because of my claustrophobia, I panicked at the very thought of walking the long underground hallway—a tunnel, really—between the gatehouse and the visiting room. The first few times I visited Carey at TSCI, I went with George Eisele, which made the long walk easier. Thereafter, I went either with Pastor David Orr or Pastor Bob Bryan, clergy sponsors of the death row Bible study, to avoid walking the tunnel alone.

A little over seven months after the move to TSCI, a bad situation became worse. Even though those on death row hadn't broken any prison rules, they were moved to the hole (January 9, 2003). Those in the general population who had been sent to the SMU, whether for violent acts or small infractions, had tele-visits; but the men on death row, who had been placed there for what Carey judged to be administrative convenience, were allowed contact visits. Nor were they to be handcuffed and shackled like the others. Even so, Carey found solitary confinement oppressive. He feared that the situation would further deteriorate if those on death row were treated like those in the general population. When those inmates were in the hole, they had to "earn" their release back to the general population and try to avoid further penalties:

> Depending on what you have done (I think), even to have your own drinking cup, you must be good for so long or not stir up trouble. Here's an example: if you talk too loud and get 6

warnings to either be quiet or keep it down, you get sent further into the hole system, or you may lose your cup or whatever else [is given] to inmates, including canteen which I assume one cannot order to[o] much of, and "yard-time" which is really a bad joke. I hate the "yard," but one cannot stay locked up 24 hours a day . . . So, in other words, you must "earn" privileges to get things and to get out of the hole (January 15, 2003).

Unlike the others, who had to go to the yard alone, those on death row could go two at a time, which allowed for human contact. Carey felt that even though those on death row had "lost a lot" of what they'd had at NSP, "I am doing my best NOT TO COMPLAIN TOO MUCH, but it's hard; and believe me—I'm praying . . . However, I know life can be even worse than what it is [. . .]. I have seen the 'Tele-visitation Room', there are four small rooms with a TV monitor & camera; we can be visiting in there; this is what we worried about when we were at NSP" (February 2, 2003).

As Carey's letters attested, the NDCS continued to rely heavily on segregation. But there was cause for hope when Director Frakes sought help in lessening his department's use of segregation from the Vera Institute of Justice, an independent nonprofit that, according to its Facebook page, works to "secure equal justice, end mass incarceration, and strengthen families and communities across America." In its 2015 Safe Alternatives to Segregation Initiative, the Vera Institute worked with five state correctional departments to reduce their use of solitary confinement. Nebraska was one of the states it chose. According to the institute's report, the daily population in any type of restrictive housing in Nebraska averaged 13.9 percent of the prison population, which was more than twice the estimated national average of 5 to 6 percent. The report recommended, among other things, increased programming, better mental health care, and adequate staffing to reduce the reliance on segregation.

Carey knew firsthand about the overuse of segregation. Many times, he had been put in solitary confinement despite committing no offenses or as punishment for what he called "the smallest of stupid infractions." For instance, Carey was sent to the hole when an inmate gave him tobacco to pass to someone else, at a time before tobacco products were banned in NDCS institutions. He remained there for two weeks until he was taken to prison court (January 13, 1999).

Of special concern is the use of solitary confinement as punishment for more than a few days, especially for inmates who are mentally ill. The prolonged isolation and lack of human contact can cause hallucinations, panic attacks, paranoia, hypersensitivity to stimuli, difficulty thinking, worsened conditions in the mentally ill, suicidal ideation, attempted suicides, and a higher suicide rate for those in solitary confinement than that of the general prison population. It also increases the rate of self-harm (cutting oneself to cause bleeding, ingesting toxins, tying a ligature around one's neck to cut off breathing, banging one's head against the wall, setting one's cell on fire). Meredith Rountree, the Northwestern University law professor who studied volunteers for execution, found that solitary confinement led to higher rates of volunteerism because such conditions so erode mental health that death seems preferable to life in isolation. Clearly, segregation is harmful, counterproductive, and costly.

Carey described prison life as a pressure cooker: men were living in such close quarters without meaningful activities to occupy their time and attention. "In my opinion, Lisa, 'Super-maximum security prisons' are conditioning inmates and staff alike to be mean & cruel to one another—and to each other. Like animals. And sooner or later, these animals will be released to society, and then what? Who will be responsible for all the damage done? This is what's happening in other 'Super-max' prisons, so why not here as well?" (February 2, 2003).

On Mother's Day, May 10, 2015, what the NDCS called an "institutional incident" erupted at about 2:30 PM at TSCI when staff released too many inmates from their housing units at once. Instead of going to the "pill line" to receive their medications, about twenty to thirty or forty inmates, depending on the source, gathered in front of Housing Units One and Two. Within twenty minutes, some inmates were disobeying orders and assaulting staff. Staff quickly lost control of the "incident"; the number of inmates involved grew to one hundred or two hundred or as many as three hundred fifty or four hundred, again, depending on the source. When staff gained control ten hours later, rioters had killed two inmates, both of whom were serving time for sexual offenses, and guards had shot two more inmates, one of whom required hospitalization. Several other inmates and staff were injured or assaulted. The cells in two living units had been ransacked, their windows were broken, mattresses set on fire, cameras pulled down and smashed, and a wall separating two units destroyed, causing about $2 million in damages.

Early reports in the media tended to present this as a random or spontaneous event. Inmates were in the wrong; staff had reacted appropriately. I read the early reports with a skeptical eye. Riots don't happen without reason, especially when one could be harshly punished not only for participating but simply for being in the vicinity of the "incident." Then, on May

12, Paul Hammel and Joe Duggan reported in the *Omaha World-Herald* that NDCS director Scott Frakes "acknowledged that one of the inmates told a media outlet that they were trying to bring a list of grievances to officials but said that he could not confirm whether that was the case."

Carey wrote frequently and at length about what he heard from staff, other inmates, and news reports about the riot, and how it affected him.

> The prison riot on the 10th was huge and expensive, causing death, injuries to both inmates & staff, damages, and more heartache & problems for all of us; most staff quit, including one female gym staff who was nearly raped. Especially staff needs our prayers. A newspaper article said that most people quit because of the prison administration, all the guff and nonsense rules for them and inmates to follow . . . I can believe it! (May 14, 2015).

A month after the turmoil, on June 10, he added that staff didn't want to work at TSCI, but because so many had quit following the riots, those that remained were required to work twelve-hour shifts, four days a week.

For several months in 2015, Carey's letters were dominated by news about the ongoing effects of the riots. Though death row had not been involved in them, he and the others celled there felt their repercussions—an aspect of the riot that received no coverage by local media that I could find. On May 14, he wrote that for several days, those on death row had been "all locked up or locked down" in their cells twenty-four hours a day, with no mail, no showers, and sacked meals. "We've been told that supper tonight will be the first hot meal (since Sunday [May] 10th lunch). We've been eating twice a day, no lunch." His thoughts leaped to future conditions. "Stupid riots! And just think . . . the death penalty may be overturned to life in prison and we'll be in the prison population with all that mess out there . . . These are uncertain times, Lisa, that's for sure" (June 10, 2015).

Carey was particularly concerned about restrictions placed on visits after the riots, and that group meetings like the death row Bible study were canceled. I had planned to join the study not long after the riot, but Pastor Bob notified me that we wouldn't be able to get in. Carey advised me to call the prison first to make sure that visits were allowed before I made the drive (May 24, 2015).

Over two months after the riots, conditions for those on death row were little improved. "Much of the prison are locked down in their cells most of the day. We are served a small hot breakfast, a sack lunch (which is a salami sandwich, small bag of chips, and fruit), and a medium sized supper. This morning around 2:30 I woke up because my stomach was growling" (July 22, 2015). I wondered if the rationale for the lockdown was preventive or punitive. And why the limited rations? A lockdown would be easier to bear if one weren't hungry.

By late July, visiting restrictions had loosened a bit, though the death row Bible study still couldn't convene as a group. Inmates, clergy, and lay clergy (I had lay clergy status) were limited to one-on-one visits, and we had to meet in the general visiting area instead of where we usually gathered, a small conference room with a long table and moveable chairs. Visits, normally three hours, were now limited to ninety minutes. Carey expressed his gratitude for our Wednesday, July 29 visit, which also included another inmate, Marco Torres, a new lay clergy volunteer, Leona Trauernicht, Pastor Bob Bryan, Carey, and me.

On August 15, Carey wrote that he and the others on death row were used to guards searching their cells twice a month, but "normally they don't tear up our cells" and search as thoroughly. Then what he dreaded happened. "Yesterday afternoon, all death row inmates were moved back to the hole (SMU or Special Management Unit), even though we haven't done anything wrong; it's a huge change for us, I am praying and doing my best not to complain and 'just go along' . . . Amen." On August 18, 2015, he wrote: "Spiritually, I am like a car, if I don't have the fuel (the Bible), getting around will be impossible."

In the same letter, Carey contextualized the riots and their aftereffects:

> I'm not sure why it has become worse here, and it seems like both inmates and staff are at fault at times; maybe it's only an escalation. I'm sure Nebraska prisons (the mentality with both inmates and staff) are behind the times of other prisons; other prisons (staff & inmates) seem more cruel, more anger and stress, so maybe we're only catching up to their normalcy of life. Or so it seems. We are certainly learning to deal with much less now, even over night.

If Carey was without a Bible at first, at some point he received one and found comfort there. "I love Phil. 4:11–13 and Heb 5:8!" In the Philippians' passage, Paul says that he has learned to be content "whatever the circumstances" by turning to God for strength. The unknown author of Hebrews says that Jesus learned obedience from his sufferings, so they weren't for naught. "It is so hard to think here with headaches that come and go," Carey reported, but he added he was "actually thankful for what little & what most I have!!! Glory be to God!" (August 18, 2015).

On September 24, Carey wrote to say that he'd heard that death row was likely to remain in segregation until November 2016, well over a year later, when Nebraskans would vote on whether to retain a legislative ban against the death penalty or to reinstate it. To his relief, in November 2015 visits were restored to near normal, though he was still in the hole.

Three different reports, two commissioned by the Nebraska Department of Correctional Services and one by the state ombudsman's office, examined the causes of what came to be known as the Mother's Day Riot. Each suggested reform.

In June, while Carey and the others on death row were in SMU cells twenty-three hours a day because of a riot they hadn't participated in, Director Frakes released a report entitled "A Critical Incident Review of the Events Surrounding the Inmate Disturbance on May 10–11, 2015." The author was Tomas Fithian, a former administrator of security and emergency management at the Washington State Department of Corrections, where Frakes had once been the deputy director of prisons. Fithian's report acknowledged that some inmates said they'd planned to introduce a set of grievances to administration. But Fithian found no evidence of such a list and gave little space to the causes of the riot. He concluded that the crisis occurred "as a matter of chance" and that the riot unfolded "when and where it did because inmates 'decided' to riot at a particular moment." This is as nonsensical as saying that the Civil War broke out not over issues or principles but "as a matter of chance," and that it unfolded "when and where it did" because Americans "decided" to go to war "at a particular moment." Fithian's recommendations focused more on how to handle a disturbance than on the systemic reforms that might have prevented it, which isn't surprising given his understanding of the event as randomly occurring. But he did suggest that NDCS and TSCI explore ways "to increase the amount of programming and idleness reducing activities available, and continue to find creative ways for a majority of inmates to participate."

In his October 20 report, state ombudsman Marshall Lux praised Frakes for calling in an outside expert to research the riot. But in his forty-eight-page analysis with twenty-three attachments, Lux reached different conclusions than Fithian and noted that Fithian's discussion of the causes of the riot "was not particularly detailed." Fithian hadn't been able to locate the list of inmate grievances, but Lux had. On the cover of Lux's report was an image taken from a TSCI video of an African American inmate, Lenaris Brown, holding a document. Because of the lighting, his face is obscured and the writing isn't decipherable. On the day of the riot, Brown held up a petition so that the associate warden, who was watching the yard, would see it. Lux says that this document is critical to one's understanding of what motivated the events of May 10. In response to Fithian's report and those prison officials that presented the riot as a random event, several inmates sent letters to the *Omaha World-Herald* explaining that what had begun as a peaceful and principled protest against prison conditions had gotten out of hand. "I'm not justifying violence," wrote inmate Terrell Thorpe, "but things aren't conceivably getting any better here b/c [because] administration is more focused on punishment versus rehabilitation." Apparently, some of the gangs at TSCI had even negotiated a truce so that, says Lux, "all of the inmates could act in concert in carrying forth the 'peaceful demonstration' on May 10." Lux said that he reported the inmates' grievances not to "ennoble" or "justify" their actions, but to understand them and so avoid another uprising. Although Lux acknowledged that any form of protest that would "disrupt the operations of a prison" wasn't an appropriate way to address grievances, he stressed that an inmate petition is a positive way of bringing attention to problems, as "More communication equals less trouble."

The list of grievances, authored by Lenaris Brown, Rashid Washington, who would be injured in the riot, and others, was comprised of eleven items. The first concerned the hole: "Administration and staff are intentionally and arbitrarily placing us in seg [administrative segregation], only to let us out again as if nothing happened." Other grievances included interference with who does and doesn't get transferred to other facilities; rewarding inmates who inform on others; the creation of two classes of inmates, one with more privileges than the other, through involvement (or lack of) with the Incentive/Wellness League; "ongoing and increasing disrespect from TSCI staff, who are becoming younger and more inexperienced as staffing problems and overcrowding become more ever prevalent"; denial of "access to modern technologies and job skills, vocational/technical training, which would prepare us for our eventual return to civilian life"; and "arbitrarily celling inmates together who aren't compatible and then denying those inmates to move into cells with an inmate they are compatible with."

I wouldn't have understood the seriousness of the problem of double-bunking incompatible inmates if Carey hadn't explained it to me. In 2018, while reflecting on the time when he feared that he might be moved from death row to life in the general population, he wrote about a former death row inmate, a volunteer for execution, who had strangled the man with whom he had been double-bunked in a solitary confinement cell intended for one. They were together there, sharing a bunk bed, television set, and toilet, twenty-three hours per day, five days a week and twenty-four hours per day on the weekends.

Before he was sentence[d] to murder and Death Row, he was at NSP, a regular inmate, for what crime I don't know, but he was in the hole and what a lousy hole! Anyway, administration was trying to get more money to build more of a hole so on purpose they threw more guys into the hole to show overcrowding, and they even doubled-up cellies; [name withheld by author] complained they better get the guy out a couple times but he wasn't listened to, so he murdered his cellie. Of course the administration blamed it all on him! Some guys in here simply do not want to be celled with another person, even if it means they will have to spend the rest of their life in prison, even in the hole, even to go nuts (or more nuts). (June 14, 2018).

Apparently, being celled with someone with whom one is extremely incompatible happens frequently enough that it was listed as one of the eleven concerns in the inmate petition of 2015.

Carey explained the breaking-point pressure that this inmate and some others experienced. "When Staff or an inmate bugs you and he or she won't stop and you simply want to be left alone, why not kill the person and be done with the aggravation—as for an example to the future possible aggravations, to prevent more problems?" (June 14, 2018). How trying it would be to be confined in a cramped space, day after day, with someone who talks constantly. Normally, if a person gets on our nerves, we can leave. But if that isn't an option and we know that nothing in the situation will be changed, could any of us say with certainty that we might not snap, too?

In his evaluation, Lux identified understaffing as a critical factor in the 2015 riot. On May 10, fifty-seven staff members were in charge of 1,024 inmates, though minimum staffing required sixty-one. Consequently, two programs and two evening recreation periods had been canceled that day. At the time of the riot, over one-third of the TSCI employees had fewer than two years' experience, which affected day-to-day operations. Lux also noted that the Corrections Emergency Response Team and Special Operations Response Team weren't assembled until three hours after they were called, as most team members lived in Lincoln or Omaha, which required a sixty- to ninety-minute commute to Tecumseh. "The real 'message' of the riot," Lux advised, "may well be that the facility needs to be repurposed in a way that makes it easier to manage given its staffing limitations."

The public wouldn't know the contents of a third report about the riot, also written in 2015, until John Wizinsky, a former inmate of TSCI, filed a lawsuit against NDCS and went to court in November 2018. Wizinsky, a diabetic who was without food and medicine for eighteen hours during the riot and was traumatized by a beating that he had witnessed, sued the prison "for failing to provide him reasonably adequate protection from rioting inmates." At the time of the trial, he still experienced nightmares and panic. His was one of several lawsuits brought by inmates or their family members against NDCS for its mishandling of the riot.

At the trial, a former TSCI warden who was being questioned asked which riot report Wizinsky's attorney, Joy Shiffermiller, was referring to. Shiffermiller didn't know that NDCS had ordered a report other than Fithian's. Attorneys representing NDCS then provided the never-before-released 2015 report about the Mother's Day Riot. In "Riot at Tecumseh State Correctional Institution: Causes, Course, and Change," Dan Pacholke, a secretary of the Washington State Department of Corrections, and Bert Useem, a professor of sociology at Purdue University, both experts on prison riots, observed that "a conjuncture of several conditions primed the institution for rebellion. The prison was under stress, inmates were unsettled, and the 'barometric pressure' was high and rising." Consequently, "small acts of resistance expand[ed] rapidly." They also saw coordinated actions from gang members that allowed them to "overwhelm staff," a different view of gang involvement than that presented by Ombudsman Lux. But like Lux, Useem and Pacholke also referred to inmate grievances and suggested that the state change the population at TSCI to what the *Lincoln Journal Star* called "lower custody inmates," which junior staff could more easily manage. Useem and Pacholke also suggested housing inmates at different custody levels so they'd have more incentive to work for lower security housing and that the prison provide more programming and rehabilitation opportunities. On December 11, 2018, the *Omaha World-Herald* reported that Frakes had not only kept this more critical study from the public but that he hadn't released relevant documents and reports requested by legislative judiciary committee chairman Senator Les Seiler and attorneys representing those who were suing the NDCS for negligence. As Paul Hammel reports in the December 11, 2018 *Omaha World-Herald*, Frakes said that he didn't release the second study "because of concerns that its revelations about organized gangs at the Tecumseh State Prison could lead to safety threats to staff, inmates and the public." In a December 7, 2018 letter to state lawmakers, Frakes explained: "In an environment like (corrections), it is . . . essential that certain information remain protected."

According to two of the three reports about the Mother's Day Riot (and Carey's letters to me), this "institutional incident" was long in the making. Following the 2015 riot, Carey wrote that nothing had improved. "I wouldn't be surprised if there's another riot here, and more deaths and injuries!" (November 17, 2015). His words were prophetic. On March 2, 2017, inmates took control of a portion of TSCI, set fires, and killed two inmates—the second deadly riot in less than two years. While Carey said little about the creation and maintenance of the prison-industrial complex at TSCI having a critical role in the development of the riots, he wrote often about how its conditions and policies affected him. The instability created by high staff turnover and understaffing. Fewer visits and Bible studies. More time in the hole. More headaches. All this and more meant that he would rather die than be moved into the general population and live under such circumstances.

Whenever something prison-related was in the news, I dreaded the comments that I'd inevitably find in letters to the editor or overhear in conversations. People often spoke about inmates as if they weren't human, as if their lives and characters weren't as complex as our own, as if they weren't like us and ours, me and mine, each "fearfully and wonderfully made" by God, as the psalmist claims. In *The Journalist and the Murderer*, Janet Malcolm observes that "The crime of murder is one we have all committed in our (conscious or unconscious) imaginations." Yet too many believe that those in prison are there because of horrifically violent crimes, the likes of which we can't imagine, much less commit. Though some of those in prison have committed heinous crimes, that certainly isn't true of all of them. Many are there because of drug offenses or crimes against property. Nonetheless, we have to "other" those in prison, to draw a hard line between them and us so we can justify confining them for months and years in substandard, even deplorable living conditions and denying them productive and meaningful ways to fill the idle hours that weigh so heavily upon them. By othering them, we don't have to question why an inmate might volunteer for execution. By othering them, we can justify isolating them in tiny cells, twenty-three hours per day and with no human contact for weeks, months, years. By othering them, we can believe that a riot occurs not as a response to intolerable, unjust conditions, but as a random, spontaneous incident because the rioters, unlike us, are unrestrained and evil and simply felt like destroying something.

# 8

# "Just Call Me Dr.-Want-to-Be-Phil"

In his contribution to National Public Radio's *This I Believe*, Troy Chapman said that his core belief is that being human means caring for others. But, said Chapman, who is serving a sixty- to ninety-year sentence at Kinross Correctional Facility in Michigan for second-degree murder, there aren't many opportunities for that in prison. "There's a lot of talk about what's wrong with prisons in America," Chapman said. "We need more programs; we need more psychologists or treatment of various kinds. Some even talk about making prisons more kind, but I think what we really need is a chance to practice kindness ourselves. Not receive it, but give it." To illustrate, Chapman explained that when a "scruffy orange cat" showed up in the prison yard, he and other inmates took turns petting her, bringing her food and water, and cutting the burrs and matted hair from her coat. And they began to have lighter, easier conversations about their visitor. By giving the inmates an opportunity to care for another creature, that cat disrupted the well-worn patterns of prison life and made them better people in the process.

Like Chapman, who wrote two books promoting what he calls "wholeness ethics," Carey also found ways to be of service while in prison. "Dr.-Want-to-Be-Phil," as he called himself—after Dr. Phil McGraw, the psychologist who dispensed advice on his syndicated television show—offered support, advice, and encouragement to those within and beyond the prison. Though Carey never married, started a family, held or lost a job, cared for an aging parent, or did many of the small, everyday things that constitute a life well lived, he was keenly interested in my experiences with these matters and offered relevant anecdotes from his life (or others') whenever he could. He managed to give sound, practical advice on such diverse topics as skipping my daughter from kindergarten to second grade (her father and I felt differently about this), whether to let Ian's girlfriend live with us so she'd be able to finish her senior year of high school (we did), or preparing myself and my children for my mother's risky neck surgery. And in many ways, he was more than qualified to help me become green and well-watered after a drought in my spiritual life. He had worked with humility and perseverance to rehabilitate himself after the big, costly mistakes of his youth; had learned to live with integrity and in relative harmony while in close, daily contact with the same group of people under highly stressful circumstances; and had prepared for his death many times only to return, once again, to "living in limbo." But more than that, he gave such wise advice to me and so many others because he was grounded in a religious philosophy and spiritual practice that required self-examination and seeking the guidance of a wise, higher power.

Carey's letters to me, especially during the early years of our correspondence, were marked by thought-provoking questions and encouragement. During the nearly three years that I lived in Carbondale, Illinois, I was heartsick that my daughter spent more time with her father than with me and her brother; I was homesick for the bigger skies and prairies of southeast Nebraska. Those few letters of mine that I saved from this time (and the snippets that Carey quoted back to me) reveal that I wrote often about my trying circumstances—enough so that upon rereading the letters, I'm embarrassed and regretful about how preoccupied I was with my own troubles. Still, the depth, insight, and sincerity in Carey's responses tell me that he relished his role as my counselor:

> When I ask you the below questions & comments, I think about things I've went through (and still am going through somewhat) in the past—well, since 1980 and since I've come to Death Row . . . This is in regard to how you've been feeling about being there in Carbondale and at the University . . . How are you talking to God about this? How do you think "He" sees you as you're pouring out your heart to Him and seeing you as you behave through all of this, like your moods and your feelings? You know what I mean, Lisa? Sometimes, sometimes we miss the glory & joy in things in "our" life and "God" wants us to see it when we are focused only on the bad—as we may see life. For instance, often (if not always) Death Row is the dreariest place, but, I'm trying (with our Father's encouragement) to see the glory & joy as He wants me to see it. Besides, this is one of the best Death

Row's in the U.S. and in the world, gosh, how would I feel if this was the worst in the U.S.?! ☺ You know what I mean? And the same could be said for you as well, yes? Of course it can. Glory be to God for what we have and for where we are from day to day, amen & amen! Please don't think I'm coming down on you, Lisa, because this is the furthest thing from my mind and not my intent; I hope & pray what I'm doing is encouraging you to see something or to see life differently... Of course I'm very sure I'm only seeing just a fraction of a whole picture, just as we can only see a speck in God's picture for our lives that pass by so quickly (I was just thinking about Bob Williams and Karla Fay Tucker), though we (sometimes?) think it is not (February 2, 1998).

Carey invited a shift in my perspective by asking me to see myself from God's vantage point. He enticed me to search for the "glory & joy" that I was missing because of my pessimism. He'd even considered that he might not be seeing my situation in full and offered his advice with humility. And he reminded me of the fleetingness of life and how fortunate we were compared to his dear friend, Bob Williams, whom the state of Nebraska had executed in December 1997, and Karla Faye Tucker, who'd been executed by the state of Texas the day before he wrote this letter. Before his powerful personal example (he was grateful to be "on one of the best death rows!"), I felt petty and ungrateful; I later told Carey that his optimism had inspired and shamed me. "I don't know if I have any, really," he answered. "I get stuck an awful lot ☺" (February 28, 1998).

Of course, Carey was right. I could change my circumstances by changing my perspective. I decided to be more intentional about savoring and celebrating the wonderful friends that my children and I had made in Carbondale. I decided that if we lived in a house that I owned rather than rented, we'd feel more invested in the place. And so, I started looking at houses and neighborhoods. But nourishing friendships and a more permanent address couldn't fix my greatest angst: being separated from my daughter. So, I applied for a few jobs closer to Lincoln and hoped for the best in a very competitive job market.

Then, in May 1998, the end of my third year at the university, I was unexpectedly offered a part-time position in teaching in an MFA program at a college in Baltimore, Maryland. Though it offered far less money than I earned at Southern Illinois University and none of the benefits, I found it desirable both because of the caliber of the students and because it was a low-residency program. Other than a couple of weeks in August when I'd had to be on campus to meet with my students, I could do my work from home—which meant that I could live anywhere. I took the job and in July,

I moved back to Lincoln and created a far better joint-parenting arrangement: every two days, Meredith alternated between her father's home and mine. Carey celebrated this with me. "Congratulations! on a new job and an ex-job and an ex-home (in Carbondale), blessings from heaven (God) does drop down to us! Hallelujah!!!" (June 20, 1998).

Carey also wrote advice-filled letters to Ian. One letter from September 30, 2004, was particularly representative of their correspondence. Carey opened with a caution about life in prison: "I'm doing okay; you know, prison life can be pretty rough every single day." He commented on Ian's choices: "I wished you had found another job before you had quit your job, or before you quit your next job. [. . .] I'm glad you're trying to find another job though, excellent!!! [. . .] I'm sure your mom can use all the help she can get (either at home or financially with all the bills that can pile up so easily)." Then, he was a cheerleader: "I know your mom is very proud of the man that is coming out of you and so am I; you should be proud of yourself as well! ☺ Keep it up!" He recommended an action: that Ian contact "Job Core." "Have you heard about this program? They train young adults in different jobs." He included the toll-free telephone number for Ian to call "if you're interested."

In the next paragraph, Carey touched on a matter that he knew was bugging me: the car sitting in my driveway that didn't run. "Your '79 Monte Carlo sounds pretty nice; try to remember that most moms don't like a car around their home that needs rebuilding, esp. if it will take a while to rebuild. ☺" And finally, he told Ian what he was reading in the Bible (Ezra) and sought, indirectly, to inspire Ian to do the same. "I have wasted so many years not reading God's word to us. But not any more, Ian." As always, he signed off: "Your friend, Carey Dean." I don't know how Ian responded to the letter, but I do know that while Ian didn't call Job Corps or read his Bible, he did get another job, he did sell the Monte Carlo, and he always counted Carey as a friend. Whenever Carey wrote to Ian, he told me what he'd said to him and why. Then he'd conclude, "Well I hope I helped—even if it's only a little bit" (December 4, 2001). I told Carey that while it's human nature to not take advice unless it aligns with what we were already inclined to do, because of the advice he gave, Ian and I thought more deeply about our options, which led to better decisions.

In the last decade of our friendship, I wrote less about work and relationships that needed "fixing" and more about making peace with matters beyond my control, like the deaths of friends and family members or matters related to aging. Carey and I usually shared news about the people we knew, anything related to the death penalty, and our spiritual lives—what we were reading in the Bible, who we were praying for, and how we dealt with our struggles with our most vexing sins like hard-heartedness, hypocrisy, and self-righteousness. But still, there were life circumstances for which he offered solutions.

In 2012, Meredith graduated from the University of Nebraska-Lincoln with a degree in music. A few months later, she moved to New York City to earn a master's degree at a music conservatory. For many months after her departure, I was at a loss as to what I should do with myself. My house seemed too big, my schedule too open.

> You wrote, "I'm wondering what's next in life for me," Why not write a book about how you've been evolving into the person you are today, and write about different problems with Ian & Meredith and how you (and they) overcame those obstacles one at a time, and your spiritual problems (with yourself and at church)? I am praying about these applications; just keep putting them in writing and pray for patience, amen ☺ (November 7, 2012).

And that is what I did: I wrote a few dozen autobiographical essays, which addressed the ways in which I was "evolving," the obstacles I encountered, and the solutions I found or created or stumbled upon or that had eluded me, as Carey had suggested. But then in 2015, as I was working on the manuscript, *Like Salt or Love: Essays on Leaving Home*, I was interrupted by the emergence of a new writing project: *Bread: A Memoir of Hunger*, about midlife eating disorders and disordered eating, including my own, a project that refused to wait its turn. I assured Carey that while it may appear that I didn't take his good advice, I seriously considered it. But then, the path that I really wanted or needed to follow pushed its way to the forefront. Without his help, I might not have gotten there. After *Bread* was published, I returned to *Like Salt or Love*. But in 2018, I was interrupted again, this time by Carey's imminent execution and my desire to write a book about our friendship. *Like Salt or Love*, the book that he had encouraged me to write, is next in the queue.

During the winter of 2017–2018, I thought seriously about selling my house and moving to Omaha so I could align both the personal and professional parts of my life in the same city. Carey assumed that I was moving because I was planning to retire soon, which wasn't the case. In fact, at that time, I'd given little thought to retiring. I was considering moving so that I could be more physically present at my job, have more opportunities to socialize with people I knew in Omaha, and live a more integrated life with my place of employment and residence in the same city. Nonetheless, his questions helped me to think through the possibilities:

> It's wonderful [you're] moving to Omaha! When will you retire? Well, your "friends" at school will change (when you retire) then

yes? And another chapter is about to be written. It seems like your retirement might be a weighing factor to your moving, yes? You'll be making new church and neighbor friends no doubt, if or when you move. What does Ian think? What's the worst thing about your house that needs repairing or replaced? What's the worst thing you see (at this time) about moving? [. . .] Well, I will be forced to change your address in my address book! That's horrifying for me! ☺ You can't move!!! Just joking ☺ What if you don't move . . . and then, you retire in a couple short years; can't your friendships grow even more than before here in church and wherever else in Lincoln? The same as in Omaha, but you're already settled here now. You wrote you felt stale . . . and I forget what else; it seems to me though that if you can't address and solve the problem or that issue today than [sic] it (these feelings) will only follow you. What do you think? I think it's possible. Just call me Dr. Want-to-be-Phil! (January 11, 2018).

Since I wanted to use the summer of 2018 to write as much of this book as possible while Carey was still alive, I had neither the time nor the desire to move. I don't regret that choice. Now, when I'm in Omaha, fifty-some miles from Lincoln, I wish that I lived there. And when I return to Lincoln, I'm glad to be here. There is no right or wrong answer to my question about where to live, though the challenges of living a geographically split life continue.

While I offered Carey words of support, only occasionally did I advise him. I didn't feel qualified to counsel him on how to deal with the stresses and dangers of prison life (with which I'd had no experience) or whether to continue or stop his appeals, and I was certain that through prayer, Bible study, and reason, he would know what to do. I tried my best to respond with sympathy and questions or provide a relevant quote from something I was reading. Even so, he found our correspondence valuable. I was pleased when he called a letter that he had written to me about his 2007 execution date "free therapy." When facing execution in 2011, he wrote, "Writing this, Lisa, has [been] a way for me to accept this, and is relaxing or soothing, just like it had [been] for me before [my execution date] in May 2007" (March 5, 2011).

Carey also served others by helping newcomers to death row become acclimated to their new "home." The abrupt change from waiting in jail during the trial to life on death row demanded huge adjustments. "Maybe you feel like everyone in the world let you down between family & friends & attorneys & the justice system, maybe you're confused, afraid, fearful, apprehensive & not trusting." Often, the newcomer just needed someone to talk to about their trial, learn what to expect in prison, or teach them how not to be taken advantage of. And sometimes, the newcomer just needed some items at the prison canteen (June 20, 2018). On September 29, 1997, Carey wrote about the arrival of "Jason" on death row:

> Gosh, he's only 23 and he looks so young & vulnerable; did I look like this when I came here at almost 23 years old? [. . .] Probaly [sic] did! Gosh, he's young! And I felt so afraid & lost about so much. He is sitting at my table in the Death Row dining room, where I sat by myself before; two guy[s] here (Pete & John) asked me to let him. It's ok with me, thank God! I'm remembering how I felt when I first came here (June 20, 1980!) and Lord willing, I can help him.

Carey and Jason became Bible study partners, memorizing the Psalms together, asking each other trivia questions, and discussing how to put into practice big theological principles like giving and receiving forgiveness. Carey was impressed by the changes he saw in his friend. "Since you don't know [Jason], believe me, the Holy spirit has been working on his stubbornness just as He works on all of us" (July 2, 1998). When I told him that "the voice of wisdom" was his and that his friend was fortunate to be the beneficiary of it, he denied it. But then he conceded that whatever he was able to do for Jason and others came from God.

Though Carey had few possessions and little money, he was generous. After I sent him a parallel Bible (a Bible with different translations of each passage arranged side-by-side) that he'd requested, he explained why he wanted it. "A couple years ago (or maybe 3), I had a parallel Bible (I forgot what versions) but then Marco Torres came on the Row and he had none (I think) so I offered something wonderful to him which he gratefully accepted. Praise God! (A part of me has always regretted that but, sharing was the most important thing to do)" (November 5, 2013). (Marco would pay forward Carey's act of kindness. When Marco saw how beat up my Bible was, he gave me one of his, which I still use.) When an inmate's TV was broken, Carey loaned him his. When a newcomer to death row needed food but had no money, Carey bought him something to eat.

He also gifted others with poetry and short prose pieces that blended autobiographical stories and Christian themes. He'd often tuck one of these in the same envelope as the letter he sent me. And he sent his poems to others as well, even though the cost of copying and postage was a sacrifice for him. Carey felt it so critical that he send his poems to his friend, "Ed," that he was willing to bear the risk and the expense.

> I wanted to send them to an old friend, [Ed], who has been in the prison's hole (called the Adjustment Center) for 10–11 years

probably. The hole is the worst place in the prison, and is 2–3 times worse than Death Row. Gosh. I feel sorry for him, and I pray real often for him. PTL! Last week, I had a copy of half of my poems made, costing $18.40, 10¢ a copy/page; I already had half of my poems copied. I did something against the rules, or actually something the prison would deny—The prison administration has inmates (6 or 7 I think) working at the prison's law library; I asked the head there if he'd mind sending my poems to [Ed] through the prison law library, and he said OK. [. . .] Well, if we get caught, then I'll say you told me to do it! Just kidding, Lisa ☺ If we get busted, then I'll face the music . . . and then I'll mail the poems (around $6.00) to Dave and he'll mail them to [Ed]. I'll find out tomorrow if we got away with this—or not (December 31, 1995).

Carey felt that it was his duty to prepare the others on death row for his execution—and their own. "I need to remind myself to be open & share my feelings and concerns with the other men on the Row, to try to help them be more accepting of our future [. . .]. I wonder what thoughts and concerns these men might have . . . I suppose I know the answer to this since I've been through it with Otey and Joubert and Bob Williams" (March 5, 2011).

Bible studies were a crucial part of these preparations. Those on death row can meet in their unit for Bible study, but to meet in a classroom in the visiting area with civilian volunteers requires a sponsoring clergy member. Creating and maintaining those study groups required prayer and persistence on Carey's part. He wrote, at his own expense, to many pastors in southeast Nebraska to inquire if they'd be willing to host the Bible study. Only a few responded to his query, and none said "yes."

> Would they as well refuse to go to visit Jesus or John or Paul in prison? I suspect so. I have no hard feelings today, and about other churches as well; I simply know that there are many churches who wants nothing to do with the rest of the family of God in prisons, there is no spirit of reconciliation, no Christ-like love for us, or rather—very little and not enough ☺ I'm sure God is willing . . . halleluyah!!! ☺ (January 27, 2011).

In 2009, Carey was involved in three Bible studies that I know of. Two of them, one with Gary and Trudy Cross and Steve Backmen and one with Bill Hance, the prison minister at the Lincoln Church of Christ, were nourishing and sustaining. "Oh, God is good to me, Lisa! Really" (December 17, 2009).

But one study was vexing. That year, a man who had once been an inmate at NSP but became a chaplain with a nonprofit prison ministry after his release began meeting with Carey and fellow death row inmate "Frank" for Bible study. Whenever Carey searched his Bible for verses related to the discussion at hand, the pastor accused him of being disrespectful and not paying attention and asked Carey to stop. Carey wrote the pastor a long, reassuring letter, but the pastor insisted that he was being rude and inattentive. Carey felt that he was not being heard and considered not attending the study anymore; at that point, he asked me for advice. "What do you think? Am I wrong?" (December 17, 2009). I suspected that the pastor's top priority was serving his ego rather than God and other people, and I told him so. I urged Carey to explain to the pastor why he was searching for passages in the Bible and to encourage the pastor to consider why that bothered him so. Ultimately, Carey and the pastor had "a serious discussion in a visit and in two letters (so far)." Frank also wrote to the pastor about his authoritarian approach (January 5, 2010). Carey admitted that it "might be a bit distracting" for participants to be looking through their Bibles and that he'd "try to cut it down"; in turn, the pastor said that he'd try to be more understanding. Because of this compromise, the Bible study was less contentious and continued for a while longer (February 15, 2010).

In 2011, Carey figured that he had two to four years left on death row before he'd leave, either through "two life sentences (slim chance but a chance nonetheless) or an execution (probably)." Before he left, he wanted to make sure that "my fellow believers have Christian visits to help them remain on a Solid Foundation. This is my prayer and hopes anyway, amen" (February 3, 2011). Although I have been an infrequent participant in these studies, I was instrumental in helping Carey find hosting pastors. He and I had started to write to each other in 1995 because his pastor could no longer visit due to his age and infirmity, and he'd needed help finding Christian fellowship. George Eisele faithfully visited Carey a couple of times a month until he moved to Kansas City about a decade later, and our pastors, Dale and Christy Dowdy, visited Carey when they could until they moved to a church in Pennsylvania in 1999. Surely my having vouched for his character was one of the reasons why they took a chance on him.

When Carey was again searching for a pastor to sponsor the death row Bible study in 2010 and 2011, I realized that I needed to vouch for him again. He had been refused or ignored by so many pastors that he abandoned the idea altogether. When I heard Pastor David Orr of First Mennonite in Lincoln speak at an event, I wondered if he might not be receptive to our request. I urged Carey to ask one more pastor before he gave up. After he'd made the initial contact with Pastor Orr, I followed up by telephone a few days later and told him of Carey's sincerity. Eventually, David said yes. Carey was jubilant. "I can hardly wait until this Friday morning (20th) which is when Pastor David Orr will hopefully be here, amen. I'll let you know how it turns out" (May 17, 2011).

After their first meeting, Carey wrote of his approval of David: "Glory be to God! Thank you so much! David is maybe 57–58 years old, has a soft voice . . . I thought we had a pretty nice time, and even got into the Word a little [. . .]. We prayed at the beginning of the visit and the end, it lasted maybe just over two hours [ . . . ]. I like David" (May 23, 2011).

The two of them met every other week for a while. "I think that because it is only me going, as it turns out (in my opinion) I think this is what David needs as well, just to get used to me a little bit; so for now, it turns out to be a blessing that only I am going" (June 15, 2011). In October, Frank joined David and Carey for a study of Romans. Eventually, six of the men on death row attended the Bible study, some regularly, some occasionally. The study was so well attended that David hosted two back-to-back sessions, as there was a limit on how many inmates could be in a classroom at the same time. I usually went to the first session; Carey attended both. One regular participant donated his artwork to Mennonite fundraisers. Another told me that should he be executed, he was leaving what little he had to David.

In 2014, David resigned from First Mennonite and took a position at a United Church of Christ in Ohio. Once again, Carey asked me to help him find a sponsoring pastor. "I will trust you (since you have the Holy Spirit) to know whom to ask to come" (March 24, 2014). At the time, I was attending worship services at two or three churches most weekends. One of those was the Saturday evening service at Our Savior's Lutheran in Lincoln. I asked Pastor Toby White if she knew of a clergyperson who might host the group, and she connected me with Pastor Bob Bryan. Because he was the director of Followers of Christ, the prison ministry of the Nebraska Synod of the Evangelical Lutheran Church in America, I didn't have to convince Bob that hosting such a study was worth his time or that an inmate's desire for a Bible study could be sincere. "I can hardly wait to meet Bob Bryan," Carey wrote on June 22, 2014. Pastor Bob's intention was to create a weekly Bible study hosted by a rotating group of lay clergy volunteers. But committing to a regular Bible study at TSCI was difficult for many of us interested in prison ministry because of the distance between Lincoln or Omaha and Tecumseh. Apart from that, both cities each had several NDCS facilities where one could more conveniently volunteer. But Pastor Bob and Leona Trauernicht, a woman in her eighties who lives thirty-five miles from Tecumseh in Beatrice, visited a couple of times a month. In 2018, Ernest Pons, who lives sixty miles from TSCI in Fairbury, joined the team, which allowed for more frequent Bible studies than Pastor Bob alone could do. When Carey was facing execution in 2018, he asked Bob to be his spiritual advisor and to witness his execution, and Bob agreed.

I've always felt blessed when I've gone to one of the death row Bible studies. As we share food from the vending machines, we get caught up on happenings in each other's lives—a difficult inmate, new prison rules, death penalty issues, health concerns (our own and that of our families), my kids and students, Bob's garden, Leona's church, Ernest's travels. Sometimes Carey selected the Bible passage for discussion; sometimes the pastor did (often Bob chose the lectionary reading that he'd be preaching on the following Saturday evening at NSP). We discussed the passage, shared our prayer concerns, laughed, prayed, and, at the beginning and end of our sessions, hugged each other. Some questions were astute, like what accounts for the different versions of the same stories in the first and second books of Kings and Chronicles? Some insights were stunning—like hearing an inmate talk about how hard it must have been for Paul, who had persecuted many and had been, if not directly, at least indirectly involved in murder, to convince people that he was a different person than the one they'd known before his conversion. When I left the sessions, I always wished that there were fewer miles between my home and TSCI so that I could have participated more often.

When I look at the box of over 320 letters that I've received from Carey and that, for some reason, I had the good sense to save, I wonder how many other people also have bundles or boxes of his warm, personal letters, how many others he coached as to the level of openness and sharing that he desired and was willing to give. Carey wrote often about his correspondents. Some were acquaintances like students who wrote to him as part of a school project, politicians, nationally known death penalty activists, or people who were just curious about him. But some were close friends who he advised about extramarital affairs, conversion from a cultlike religion to mainstream Christianity, credit card debt, pride, grief, drug use, the fallout from issues raised by the settling of a family inheritance, and so much more. On at least one occasion, he helped someone else write a letter. When the marriage of Dave and his wife was on the rocks, Carey counseled them in hopes that they could stay together. He spent seven days typing the fourteen-page handwritten letter that Dave had written to his wife. "This may be his [Dave's] last chance to try to work out marital problems, which surely at times seems to worsen. If Dave gives his letter to [his wife] I hope it has a healing touch to it" (May 8, 1998). I wrote to him that if he "ever got out of that place," he should consider becoming a marriage counselor.

Writing so many letters was a hefty expense for him. "Death Row inmates receives (5) 'FREE' stamped envelopes each month (although we need to request it each month or else we won't get it) and finally (last night) I received mine, praise God!" (May 20, 2011). He kept meticulous records of the postage that I bought him with money orders, as I couldn't send cash or stamps. "In regards to 'prestamped envelopes', you sent me a $5 M/O [money order] on July 1, 1999. Since then I have written you 18 letters, which is $6.48. I keep forgetting to ask you to send me another $5 M/O to help me buy prestamped envelopes? ☺ Oooops, this is #19, so it is actually $6.84. If possible, Lisa, thank you so much!" (November 19, 2000). When a correspondent wasn't willing to contribute to postal expenses after several requests, Carey would explain that he couldn't afford to keep writing to them and stopped.

Though he never left death row, Carey created many opportunities to serve others. How many more people could he have helped had his life turned out differently? He might have been an excellent pastor, therapist, life coach, or ombudsman. Maybe he could have been the host of his own television program in which he gave his direct, commonsense advice to many millions of viewers.

"This is my advice free of charge! ☺" (May 8, 1999).

# 9

## "Waiting for Some Sort of Outcome"

We wait—for the arrival of true love, the graduation, the finalizing of the divorce, the life we always thought we'd have. And, too, there are the small, daily waits—for news, a paycheck, for the night to end, for a pain to pass, for better weather. Carey anticipated the arrival of many of the same things that most of us do. But some of his waits—to hear whether a scheduled execution would be carried out or postponed and, if carried out, by electrocution or poisoning—were beyond my imagining. "Will 'Death Row' be leaving the hole any time soon?" he wrote on September 15, 2016. "We aren't sure. Not until November of course but after that, we don't know. A whole lot of waiting. A lot of wasted years, Lisa."

Because the electric chair was Nebraska's sole means of execution until it was outlawed in 2008, Carey long referred to being executed as "taking the chair." Between 1920 and 1997, a total of fifteen men were executed in Nebraska; Carey knew three of them. The last, Bob Williams, was a cherished friend of his. The most famous person to die in what Carey called "Old Sparky" was mass murderer Charles Starkweather. His murder spree and 1959 execution inspired movies such as *Badlands* and *Natural Born Killers*; the title piece of Bruce Springsteen's album, *Nebraska*; and Christian Patterson's photobook, *Redheaded Peckerwood*.

On several occasions, Carey said that he wanted to die, but that didn't mean that he wasn't afraid. As most media coverage of executions provided details about the physical aspects of execution (for example, the first jolt of electricity that might or might not render the inmate unconscious as alternating currents ripped through his organs, causing his flesh to burn and his body parts to burst into flames), had I been in Carey's position, I might have forbidden myself to read such reports. The new protocol that the NDCS was to have used to kill Carey in 2007 called for "a single 20-second, 2,450-volt jolt" instead of what it had used to kill Wili Otey, John Joubert, and Bob Williams (2,450 volts for eight seconds, followed by 480 volts for 22 seconds, a sequence that was repeated after a 20-second pause). According to the coroner's reports, Joubert and Williams both were blistered after their executions, and Williams's body was "charred on both sides of a knee and the top of his head." One witness reported that Otey was still breathing after the first two jolts. Supposedly, the new electrocution protocol was more humane.

I vividly remember reading the gruesome details of the May 26, 1979 execution of John Arthur Spenkelink in Florida's electric chair. After capital punishment was reinstated in the United States in 1976, Spenkelink was the first person to be unwillingly executed (Gary Gilmore, the first to be willingly executed, had chosen a firing squad as his means of death). When I reread articles about Spenkelink's execution today, I'm struck by how accurately I remember one detail in particular: that the skin below the electrode cuff on his right leg had been split and seared. I remember how disturbing I'd found the other details the first time I read them: the fear in Spenkelink's eyes; the hood that would cover them; the three surges of electricity; the smoke that rose in the execution chamber; the curling and blackening of his hands. What I hadn't recalled were details about the behavior of the crowd outside the prison. Opponents chanted "Government murder! Government murder!" while proponents chanted "Fucking murderers!" and held signs saying "GO SPARKY." But nothing there was as savage as what I'd seen and heard at Otey's execution. When I'd read and reread the horrific details of Spenkelink's execution in 1979, I was ashamed and puzzled that I, a pacifist and opponent of the death penalty, was so engrossed by them. Perhaps it was then that I first realized that executions appealed to something in humans that I couldn't identify and didn't want to own: an excitation at seeing something so barbarous; a curiosity about what happens to the human body when mortally wounded; a need to know how another person faces a brutal, calculated death and, by extension, how I might face my own.

Carey was to have been executed by Nebraska's new electrocution protocol on May 8, 2007. Some experts feared that with this procedure, the heart of the condemned might restart or continue beating after the first jolt. But his execution was stayed because the NDCS hadn't followed a state law requiring public hearings and state oversight when devising its electrocution protocol. On February 8, 2008, the Nebraska Supreme Court ruled in an appeal brought by Nebraska death row inmate Raymond Mata (*State v.*

*Mata)* that the state's new procedure violated the prohibition in the Nebraska constitution against cruel and unusual punishment. Nebraska, which had the dubious distinction of being the only state with electrocution as its sole means of execution, would have to find another way to kill its condemned.

"What's happening in my appeals today?" Carey wrote on May 19, 2008. "Well, Lisa, because we know [sic] longer have the Chair, my last argument was about the changing of the method of execution that NSP changed to, but now, no Chair and all my arguments are completely legally exhausted." But Alan Peterson claimed that if Nebraska legalized lethal injection, his client could argue that because he had been sentenced to die in the electric chair, he could not be killed by another means, like a lethal injection. Carey judged this to be a "small" argument and predicted that others on death row would also use it. But he was tired of waiting and eager for the state to decide how he was to be put to death: "Early 2009 maybe all the Senators/legislators will vote on lethal injections; oh, Lisa, I hope they vote one way or the other" (August 4, 2008).

His hope was fulfilled. On May 28, 2009, Governor Dave Heineman signed into law LB 36, which changed the state's method of execution from electrocution to lethal injection. But because of continuing questions about the drug protocol and difficulties with legally obtaining the drugs, nine years would pass before the state would kill an inmate by that method.

LB 36 was patterned after Kentucky's three-drug lethal injection law, which, according to a 2008 Supreme Court ruling, did not violate the Eighth Amendment, which forbids the inflicting of "cruel and unusual punishments." The first drug under the Kentucky protocol was sodium pentothal, an anesthetic that induces unconsciousness and blocks pain. The second drug, pancuronium bromide, paralyzes the muscles and halts respiration. Because this drug is exceptionally painful when it enters the bloodstream, it must be administered immediately after the sodium pentothal. Finally, potassium chloride is administered to stop the heart. But because improper administration of the drugs causes excruciating pain, courts around the country have had to consider whether this protocol might violate an inmate's Eighth Amendment rights.

Carey closely followed the lethal injection debate in Nebraska and elsewhere. On October 29, 2010, he wrote that a few states were trying to work around a nationwide shortage of one lethal injection drug by using only one or two drugs to kill the condemned. If Nebraska sought to do the same, he'd probably have grounds for appeal. "I'm not quite sure how I feel about the drug shortage but, praise God, He knows what is truly best for each of us; and besides, 50 years from now it simply won't matter what happens today to us, probably in 25 years as well! ☺ Maybe 10 years! Or five!"

Four months later, Carey still hadn't received any news about how or when the state intended to kill him, and he didn't expect the situation to change soon. "I'm guessing that (at the very least), I'll be blowing in the wind for at least 4 or 5 months—very possibly longer (if the A.G. or NSP can't borrow the Thiopental from another State or switch to a different name drug). I don't know. It doesn't matter; I mean, Lisa, I've been blowing in the wind for the last 31 years in the Supreme Cts, wherever our Lord blew me to. No kidding! ☺" (February 24, 2011).

On April 21, 2011, the Nebraska Supreme Court (NSC) set a June 14 execution date for Carey. But later that month, the Drug Enforcement Administration confiscated Nebraska's supply of sodium pentothal: because the state didn't have a license to import it, it had been illegally obtained. "Underhanded secrets," Carey called this (July 7, 2011). And so, the NSC was forced to postpone his execution. On September 20, Carey wrote that Attorney General Jon Bruning's "deception of not actually having the 1st of the 3 drug cocktail will be raised very thoroughly in every Supreme Ct we go into; oh, the A.G. still doesn't have the 1st of the 3 drugs needed. You can be sure when they do, they'll announce it from heaven to hell . . . You are right, the A.G. must be disciplined or held accountable in some way; Jerry's [Soucie] attention is focused on that big-time but mine not so much."

On October 25, the NDCS acquired a supposedly legal supply of sodium pentothal. The NSC set an execution date, not for Carey but for Michael Ryan. Again, the court issued a stay because of concerns about how the drug had been obtained. On November 22, 2011, Prithi Kochhar, the CEO of Naari AG, a Swiss pharmaceutical company, wrote to the NSC chief justice, Michael Heavican, and Nebraska Attorney General Bruning that his company had given the sodium pentothal to Chris Harris, a Calcutta-based middleman, who'd said that it would be used as an anesthetic in Zambia. When Naari AG learned that Harris had sold the drug to Nebraska for use in executions, the company requested that it be returned.

On May 17, 2012, Carey wrote of a long conversation that he'd had with Jerry Soucie concerning the motion his attorney was submitting on his behalf to the state supreme court regarding how and when the NDCS had purchased one of the three drugs, including its use of a middleman. Bruning had ten days to "file an argument to my Motion." Then, the motion would go to court. "The Court may give me a 'Temporary Stay' until they decide, or they may of course decide right away if there's no weight to my Motion. Actually, I think the Motion Jerry wrote is a very good one." But again, Carey was so conflicted about whether to fight or volunteer for execution that he almost didn't sign it.

For the next several years, Carey waited for some sort of outcome as the NDCS continued searching for legal sources of drugs, and the court challenges continued. As in Nebraska, so were these battles waged in other death penalty states. Major pharmaceutical companies were putting measures in place to block the sale of their products to prisons, arguing that because their mission was to improve the quality of life, they couldn't allow their products to be used to kill people. Pfizer's 2017 statement is typical: "Pfizer makes its products to enhance and save the lives of the patients we serve. Consistent with these values, Pfizer strongly objects to the use of its products as lethal injections for capital punishment." Of course, these companies also made sure to stress that this wasn't to be understood as their position on the rightness or wrongness of capital punishment. Regardless, their new restrictions ended the open market for execution drugs, which made it increasingly difficult for states to obtain the lethal drugs.

As execution drugs became harder to obtain, states began to experiment with new formulas. "I heard a couple days ago that a State (I forgot which one) switched to a one drug Lethal execution, the drug that was given to Michael Jackson . . . I was surprised! It is rumored that (if) the A.G. acts today that it may take 9 to 12 months to change the first of the three drugs given to any of us" (June 4, 2012). In 2012, Missouri intended to use propofol, the drug that Carey had spoken of, to execute people. Prior to 2009, most states had a three-drug execution protocol. Then, eight states moved to a one-drug protocol that involved a lethal dose of anesthetic. In 2018, Nebraska was the first state to use fentanyl as one of four drugs used to carry out a death sentence. That, of course, was Carey's. Legal challenges followed. And as states increasingly turned to questionable or outright illegal means of acquiring drugs and bungled executions began to draw scrutiny and condemnation, many states found ways to shield their execution-related activities from the public. According to the Death Penalty Information Center, between January 1, 2011 and August 31, 2018, legislatures in thirteen states (including Nebraska) developed secrecy statutes that barred the public from obtaining information about how executions were carried out. Such laws undermined the efforts of the drug companies "to protect the integrity of their products" and their reputations.

One of the NDCS's "secrets" was the source of the four drugs that it used to execute Carey. Director Frakes contended that confidentiality laws protected such information from being made public. In response, the *Omaha World-Herald*, the *Lincoln Journal Star*, and the ACLU of Nebraska successfully challenged this claim in court. On May 15, 2020, the Nebraska Supreme Court ordered the NDCS to release documents about the drugs, including "purchase orders, chemical analysis reports, communications with the supplier, DEA forms, invoices, inventory logs and a photograph of the packaging," according to the *Omaha World-Herald*. On July 23, 2020, the news broke that the NDCS had purchased the drugs for $10,500 from Community Pharmacy Services in Gretna, the company that had managed the pharmaceutical operations for the Nebraska correctional system from 2016 to 2018. Immediately, Kyle Janssen, the owner of Community Pharmacy, expressed regret for having supplied the execution drugs.

Secrecy also surrounded Carey's execution: in the death chamber, the NDCS closed the curtains for fourteen minutes so that witnesses couldn't observe what was happening. Director Frakes said that this was necessary to avoid disclosing the identities of the members of the execution team to the public. In 2019, State Senator Patty Pansing Brooks introduced a bill (LB 238) that required two state senators to witness an execution from the time the condemned inmate entered the execution chamber until he was pronounced dead. During that time, the witnesses were to have an unobstructed view of the process. "We are not going to sit and let the government tell us, 'Trust us, we did it properly.' If that's so, then let us watch and make sure that that is happening properly," Pansing Brooks explained. In February 2020, LB 238 received first-round approval by a vote of 33–7. Governor Ricketts vetoed the bill.

The media updates about these matters were often dull and technical, even to one such as me, who had a friend and several acquaintances who'd be directly affected by whichever poisons the state injected into their veins, under what circumstances, and by whom. But Carey's interest in these details was keen and practical. "I'm trying to be patient and wait for next Friday (30th), when the A. G. will have the first of 3–4 'Public Hearings' on changing the Lethal injection drugs . . . I hope to hear something about the list of names who they'll request executions on. 'Help me be more patient, Lord'" (December 25, 2016).

This was a wait filled with hope and despair.

Senator Ernie Chambers, a stalwart opponent of capital punishment, had introduced a bill to abolish Nebraska's death penalty every year since 1976, his first year in the unicameral. The only exception was 2009–2012, when recently enacted term limits forced him to sit out a term before being reelected. Most years his repeal bill was indefinitely postponed in committee or on General File. But twice it came close to becoming law. In 1979, the bill passed, though it was vetoed by Governor Charles Thone. In 2007, the legislature came within one vote of passing it. Then in May 2015, during

Chambers's thirty-seventh attempt at abolishing Nebraska's death penalty and replacing it with a life sentence, something extraordinary happened. The unicameral passed LB 286 on a vote of 32–15 and overrode Governor Peter Ricketts's veto by a 30–19 margin. This was remarkable because Nebraska's officially nonpartisan unicameral is dominated by Republicans. The repeal was achieved through a coalition of Democrats, one libertarian, and libertarian-minded Republicans who defeated the more typical "tough-on-crime" Republicans. Nebraska was the first red state to abolish the death penalty.

I wasn't present for the 2015 debate or the vote. But during the debate on Chambers's 2013 bill, which also would have changed a death sentence to life in prison, I sat in the balcony of the legislative chamber with other death penalty opponents wearing white, the color of abolition. Also there supporting passage of the bill was Mariam Thimm Kelle, whose brother James Thimm, and five-year-old Luke Stice, the son of another cult member, had been tortured and murdered by cult leader Michael Ryan. I heard speeches from senators who were eloquent and well-informed; I heard speeches from senators who were woefully ignorant of the issues. Chambers's bill died when supporters weren't able to gather enough votes to end the filibuster against it. Even so, this was a bit of a victory, as it was the first time since 1979 that most senators had appeared willing to vote for abolition.

Carey also followed the debate and the vote. In 2013, he wrote, "Well, there is still a death penalty (this year) and I think it shocked Ernie that he wasn't able to pass it this time. [. . .] It certainly seemed like we wouldn't have the death penalty any longer and I was nervous about this. Change I guess" (May 29). A few months later, Carey wrote to Senator Scott Lautenbaugh of Omaha, one of the leaders of the filibuster and an enthusiastic supporter of capital punishment, whom the *Lincoln Journal Star* reported as saying, "Some people have earned the ultimate penalty that the state can mete out. There is a point at which we all have an obligation to stand our ground." Lautenbaugh said that he never regretted an execution being carried out. "I won't shed a tear and I won't mourn, except for the passage of time. I cannot have sympathy for these men on death row. They have forfeited their right to be part of the human race."

The main point in Carey's letter to Lautenbaugh was "'Get to work' and pass the right bills for the death penalty in the 2014 session year . . . even if that means substituting the Topental they can't get a hold of or going to either a two drug or a one drug execution like other states has [sic]." Another death row inmate also wrote to Lautenbaugh about the need to pass a lethal injection bill. His letter "was so much worse than mine," meaning that Carey had likely found it blunter and more forceful (July 17, 2013). Carey didn't mention if he heard back from Lautenbaugh, though, given the senator's view that those sentenced to death aren't human beings, I doubt that he'd felt compelled to answer.

When I heard the news in 2015 that LB 286 had passed and that capital punishment was no longer legal in Nebraska, I was shocked and overjoyed, and some of my abolitionist friends and I shared our happiness on social media. I regretted not having been there to witness the vote. Like Carey, I'd followed the debate through newspaper and television coverage. Senator Colby Coash of Lincoln, who had been one of those supporting Otey's execution on that awful night in 1994 but had changed sides on the issue because of the behavior displayed by the pro-death penalty crowd, had been instrumental in gathering conservative support for the measure. "This is a vote on character, and now is the time to be strong," he advised his colleagues. "Now is the time to be statesmen, not politicians." When Senator Pansing Brooks asked her colleagues, "Do you believe in the sanctity of a human soul or not? Which of you can say that a human soul cannot change and thereby never be of any value ultimately to God?" she seemed, to me, to be speaking with Carey in mind. Senator Robert Hilkemann of Omaha had voted for repeal but was undecided about the veto. In the end, Hilkemann felt that he couldn't support what he saw as a failed policy. "I really feel the Lord put me down here for a reason and maybe this was the reason," he said. "I feel I represented my district well today."

For other senators, casting a vote was difficult; they seemed to want to support repeal but because that conflicted with the desires of their constituents, they sustained the governor's veto. "This has been the hardest issue that I have confronted during my time here in the Unicameral," John Murante of Gretna said. "I pledged to do my best to vote the way the majority of my constituents want, and it has become obvious to me that the majority support Gov. Ricketts' veto."

On May 24, Carey wrote that he and others on death row had watched the debate on television, even though they had trouble picking up the station. He found the debate interesting but wasn't enthusiastic about repeal. As awful as death row was, there were aspects about life in the general population that he found worse. He felt that staff tended to treat those on death row better than those in the general population. This was likely because death row is a small and relatively unchanging group of people, which makes it safer and more predictable, relatively speaking. Carey believed that a life sentence would not only increase his suffering but would eliminate his two most likely possibilities of leaving prison: an overturned sentence or an execution. He dreaded the thought of sharing a cell (death row inmates have their own cells) because of the difficulties mismatched cellmates faced.

He would miss visits with Nebraskans Against the Death Penalty, a group that would probably disband if the death penalty were abolished. Besides all that, being in the general population would also be more expensive for him. "Here on the Row, we lend each other things from the canteen, but not in the population; in population [...] it's a different mentality" (May 15, 2013). With a life sentence, he might have to pay reparations to the families of his victims. He never said that he opposed such a plan; on the contrary, his concern was how he'd pay for it. More than once he said that if he was moved to the general population, he hoped for a job in the laundry because it offered guaranteed work and pay, though he'd heard that it was a slow, difficult process to get a job there. I assumed that being able to participate in worship services would balance out some of the negatives, but I was wrong. "A lot of inmates go to the Sunday service to hang out, so there's lots of talking & laughing and the homosexuals go to meet up." Similarly, when those from the general public with visiting privileges participated in worship services, "many guys (inmates) go to try to pick up women" (May 24, 2015).

When I first learned that Carey and several others on death row didn't want life sentences, I was surprised. But theirs isn't an uncommon response to such a change. When Illinois Governor George Ryan commuted 160 death sentences to life sentences in 2003, several inmates fought their commutations, believing that they "decreased their chances of getting new trials or reduced sentences," according to a *Chicago Tribune* report by Rudolph Bush and Steve Mills. They preferred death row because there, their cases received more scrutiny from activists, attorneys, and state-funded investigators, who fought to overturn their convictions or reduce their sentences. There were also some emotional factors. Bush and Mills report that those on death row had "a certain closeness born of their common circumstances," a "camaraderie among the condemned," so to speak, and they experienced "a sort of celebrity among those devoted to abolishing the death penalty."

Many experts agree that replacing a death sentence with life without the possibility of parole, as Chambers's bill did, wouldn't improve the conditions in which the inmate lived because he would remain in death-row-like circumstances without the legal channels a death sentence provided. In *Death and Other Penalties: Philosophy in a Time of Mass Incarceration*, Andrew Dilts writes that for the death-sentenced, "the Court requires strict review of offender qualifications, strict procedural guidelines, extended appeals processes, and additional standards of heightened scrutiny." The same level of protections is not there for those with other types of sentences. Carey had heard rumors along such lines about what awaited him should the repeal bill survive the 2016 referendum vote. "About the Death Penalty . . . I hear that even if Capitol [sic] Punishment is repealed in November, that we will still be on Death Row except without the punishment to be carried out on us. I'm not sure what to think of that if that is true; it's like being on Death Row until natural death occurs" (January 9, 2016). And yet, I wondered if it wouldn't be some kind of relief to know that one wasn't living under a death sentence and always waiting—for the outcome of an appeal, a vote in the state legislature, a veto, an execution date, a stay. Always waiting.

Even though the death penalty had been repealed, Carey and the others on death row would not see their sentences commuted. In response to the repeal, death penalty proponents formed Nebraskans for the Death Penalty, to which Governor Ricketts and his father, billionaire and TD Ameritrade founder Joe Ricketts, made hefty contributions. In the summer and early fall of 2015, members of that group gathered enough valid signatures on a petition drive to suspend LB 286 and preserve the death penalty until the public could vote on it. An unsuccessful lawsuit filed on behalf of longtime abolitionists Richard and Christy Hargesheimer sought to cancel the referendum vote because Governor Ricketts, who was "the primary initiating force" for the measure, hadn't included himself on the list of sponsors as was required by state law. But District Court Judge Lori Maret ruled that the governor wasn't required to identify himself as a sponsor and struck down the lawsuit. On November 8, 2016, 61 percent of Nebraska voters chose to overturn LB 286, thus retaining capital punishment in Nebraska. Though Carey was overjoyed, he wrote on August 8 that he felt sorry for those on my side of the issue.

Like me, most of my friends and acquaintances voted to retain the repeal. But the few people that I spoke with who had voted to restore capital punishment didn't know that a life sentence without parole in Nebraska really did mean that the convicted wouldn't be leaving prison. Nor did they know that a life sentence is much cheaper than a death sentence. In a 2016 study, Ernest Goss, a professor of economics at Creighton University in Omaha, estimated that *each* death penalty prosecution costs Nebraska taxpayers about $1.5 million more than that of a life sentence without parole. Surely, the vote would have turned out differently had voters been educated about what exactly the death penalty would be replaced with and how much money taxpayers would save if capital punishment was abolished.

Although the outcome of the election gave Carey some hope, he was still waiting. "But now, I'll probably have a long wait for the new Lethal injection drugs or for the search for the same old drugs" (November 10, 2016).

In 2017, one year after Nebraska voters restored the state's death penalty, the American Civil Liberties Union of Nebraska initiated a lawsuit on behalf of those on death row. The ACLU argued that because Nebraska was without a death penalty from August 30, 2015, when repeal went into effect, and October 16, 2015, when the signatures on the referendum that would force a statewide vote on the repeal were counted and verified, the sentences of those on death row had been converted to life sentences. Eight inmates joined the lawsuit; three did not. "Jeff [Hessler], Art [Gales], and myself are called the 'Indispensable Party Defendants' since we are not with the Plaintiffs (other Death Row inmates)," Carey wrote on December 22, 2017. Later, the ACLU would argue that Carey's execution should be postponed until its lawsuit was decided. The court rejected both of the ACLU's claims.

Because I thought that the ACLU had at least a small chance of winning its lawsuit, I gently encouraged Carey to join the other plaintiffs, even though I knew that he wouldn't and why. "This month will be my 37 1/2 years on the Row, and anytime over 10 years on the Row is LONG; and I think joining that lawsuit will only 'slow things up' maybe." He feared the lawsuit would be appealed to higher and higher courts, delaying the ultimate decision for many years. "No more procrastination. I made that mistake with Alan Peterson, allowing him to do this or that and I am still here, I'm sorry but, I don't want to be" (December 5, 2017).

I didn't try to persuade him again.

To be always "waiting for some sort of outcome" for something as consequential as if, when, or how one will be put to death, takes a tremendous toll on the body and mind. Writing in the *New Republic*, Stephen Lurie says that prisoners on death row face unique existential stress from "living under an ever-present sentence of death, with much of this time spent not knowing when the actual execution will take place. [. . .] Numerous courts, including the Supreme Court of California and the Inter-American Court of Human Rights, have found that the wait for execution 'terrorizes' prisoners and thus constitutes cruel, inhuman, and degrading treatment." Consequently, over one in ten inmates volunteer for execution—though there are many waits involved with that, too. Others seek a more certain way out, which is one of the reasons the suicide rate on death row is about six times that of the general prison population and about ten times that of the entire US population.

And, too, the wait for execution is much longer than it used to be. Charles Starkweather was executed in Nebraska's electric chair seventeen months after his killing spree. But Lurie reports that between 1984 and

2015, the time between an individual's sentencing and his execution has almost tripled, from an average of six to fifteen-plus years. During Carey's thirty-seventh year on death row, a guard searched online to discover which death row inmate in the United States had been held the longest. "It's me!" Carey wrote on February 22, 2017. "I thought maybe there were 2–3–4 others ahead of me." Actually, Carey was correct. A few others had lived with death sentences longer than he had. Raymond Riles has been on death row in Texas since 1976, but in 2021, a Texas court threw out his sentence, as the jury had not been given instructions to consider his mental illness as a mitigating factor. Riles is waiting to be resentenced. In 2013, Gary Alvord died of natural causes in a Florida prison after thirty-nine years on death row. But certainly, Carey came close to setting the national record.

The most anguishing kind of wait is that of the powerless, who have no way to hurry the news or the arrivals and departures. Carey was always waiting for other people to make life-and-death decisions for him, as well as enduring the smaller waits involved in living in a prison where your schedule is not your own. Irish essayist and novelist Edna O'Brien writes that "the secret of the sickness or non-sickness of waiting" depends on whether the wait is founded on hope or despair. Those waits that Carey endured were marked by both.

# 10

## The Outcome

Friday, August 10

Carey anticipated that one week prior to his August 14, 2018, execution date, he'd be transported from the supermax in Tecumseh to the Nebraska State Penitentiary in Lincoln, where the execution chamber was. There, he'd be on death watch, those days just before an execution when the execution team completes its preparations and the condemned is closely monitored so that he can't kill himself and deprive the state of that opportunity. Because I didn't want to miss my chance to see him when he was at NSP or the sweet, consoling companionship that I'd had with others protesting the execution at the noon vigils in front of the governor's mansion, I considered postponing a long-planned trip to visit Meredith at her home in New York City from August 4 through 10. "Stay in Lincoln," she'd advised. "Carey Dean's execution happens once; you can come to see me anytime." But Carey told me otherwise. "You should go to NYC, go! Really ☺. You'll be back in time!" (July 25, 2018). So, I went. I arranged for the woman who tended to my cats while I was away to photograph and text me any letters that I received from Carey during this time so I could promptly answer them. In his August 3 letter, he wrote that he might be moved at any time during the week prior to his execution "even possibly on the 10th" and that I was one of about thirty on his list of visitors. He anticipated liberal visiting hours.

It was good to be in Brooklyn with Meredith. I helped her hunt for a new apartment, went to a couple of her performances (she's a professional violinist), and wandered around the Brooklyn Museum with her. This constant stream of activities and companionship kept me from thinking about the looming execution as often as I would have, had I stayed in Lincoln. Even so, every day I was in New York, I checked the online edition of the *Lincoln Journal Star* and the Nebraska NPR station for news about the execution. At that point, I believed that there was still a better than even chance that it would be stayed, given the many questions concerning the legality of Nebraska's drug protocol. Nebraska's four-drug combination—diazepam, a sedative; fentanyl, a narcotic painkiller; cisatracurium besylate, which would relax or paralyze Carey's muscles and stop his breath; and potassium chloride, which would cause cardiac arrest and severe pain—had never been used in an execution. On August 7, the German drugmaker Fresenius Kabi sued to block the execution, suspecting that NDCS had illegally obtained two of the drugs that the company manufactured. But because the NDCS was refusing to reveal how it had acquired the cisatracurium besylate and potassium chloride, the company couldn't know for sure. Fresenius Kabi was concerned that the cisatracurium besylate might not work as expected because state documents suggested that corrections staff hadn't stored it at the proper temperature. The company also claimed that Nebraska's lethal use of drugs intended to save and enhance lives would damage its business and its reputation. This pending lawsuit, which seemed solid enough to me to halt or delay the execution, may have been the reason that the NDCS hadn't yet transferred Carey from TSCI to the Lincoln prison. But on Friday, August 10, US District Court Judge Richard Kopf denied a temporary restraining order against the execution, claiming that Fresenius Kabi's reputation would not be harmed if its drugs were used to end a life. The execution could proceed.

Carey and I both arrived in Lincoln on the evening of the tenth, I by airplane from New York, he shackled in a prison van.

## Saturday, August 11

At the front desk, a guard led me through a locked door and up a flight of stairs to an elevator, then guided me through a maze of locked doors and hallways until we walked past three armed guards—one standing, two sitting—and turned left. In a room at the end of the final hallway, the guard repeated the pat-down she'd done just minutes earlier at the front desk, just in case I'd acquired contraband during our trek. I wondered if this was the room where Carey was staying, since the narrow bed, though made, looked as if it had been slept in. We returned to the guards. In the room just beyond them, Carey sat in a chair at an overbed hospital table with an empty chair across from him and a stainless-steel toilet on the wall behind him. "I seen you walk past!" he said, beaming. I was his first visitor. He stood, and we hugged each other.

"I am so sorry this is happening to you. Not just this"—I waved my arm around the almost bare room—"but everything."

"Oh," he said softly, thoughtfully. Then his tone brightened. "I'm all right. Really!"

We sat across from each other. He'd lost weight since I'd seen him two months earlier. Far from the tidy, buttoned-up, tucked-in appearance I was used to, he wore a white T-shirt that hung loosely from his shoulders, tan pants, and rubber slip-on sandals with white socks. He leaned forward and rested his forearms on the table.

After he was transferred to TSCI in 2002, the only times I'd seen him were either at Bible study, where he was one of several sitting around a table, or as part of a small group in the gymnasium-like visiting room. It had been a long time since I'd looked him in the face with such directness and scrutiny. His eyes were intensely blue and steady behind wire-rimmed glasses. The top of his head was bald; the hair at the sides was short, thin, and blond. His face was rounder than it used to be, and his skin was smoother than mine; but then, I'd spent far more time in the sun than he had. His nails were clean and clipped, though not short. He looked happy.

On August 11, the pharmaceutical company Sandoz, Inc. filed a brief requesting that Nebraska reveal the source of its cisatracurium besylate. Carey was relieved when Judge Kopf said that he wouldn't decide that case until after the execution date. "When I heard that the judge denied the drugmaker's request, I shouted, 'Praise God!' four times. My hands were in the air," he said as he demonstrated. "'Praise, God!' I guess I was so loud that Art heard me." (Arthur Gales was in the cell next to his.) For Carey, the door was now open and the way clear. He marveled that on the morning of August 14, he would finally see Jesus.

Because I'd been interviewed by the *Lincoln Journal Star* and an Omaha TV station about my friendship with Carey and my thoughts on his execution, several people had contacted me through Facebook with messages for or about him. Christy Dowdy, who pastored with her husband Dale at my former church, requested Carey's address so they could write to him. A friend of a woman that Carey had dated at the time of the murders wished him well. One of George Eisele's daughters told me that despite her father's Parkinson's disease and other health problems, he'd heard about Carey's imminent execution. A grandson of Reuel Van Ness Jr. shared that he and a few others in his family had forgiven Carey:

> I don't know if you'll ever talk to Carey Dean again, but if you do, feel free to let him know that I've forgiven him. I'm certain my father has, and my oldest sister. There has been pain involved in just being related to it, and it wasn't always easy especially reading up on the incident, but I know how important forgiveness is, and how fulfilling and relieving it is to forgive and to be forgiven. So, if you do get to talk to him, please do let him know that I forgive him.

"Well, praise God!" Carey said when he heard each message. I told Van Ness's grandson that if Carey got a stay, he should consider writing to him.

"If I get a stay," Carey said with dismay. "I hope that God . . ." He paused. "I hope that God keeps the door open and pulls me through."

When I first met Carey, he often stuttered, which he attributed to the fear he had felt as a child towards his father. But in recent years, he didn't seem to stammer as much. He spoke slowly and deliberately; sometimes he'd say "no," back up, start again, and correct himself, or pause mid-sentence to center himself.

"I can't imagine what this waiting must be like for you," I said.

"I've had a lot of practice," he said flatly.

We sat in silence for several minutes. The window in the room opened onto a view of Nebraska Highway 2, the Nebraska Department of Transportation building, and the parking lot where on September 1 and 2, 1994, I'd stood with about two thousand other people. Those of us who opposed that execution waved our candles at the window—perhaps this one—where Wili Otey raised his shackled hands and waved back. Then, the room went dark and he was gone. Otey's appeal with the US Supreme Court was denied at 7:55 PM; he was executed just after midnight on the second of September. Carey, however, didn't want a last-minute reprieve. Nor did he want anyone protesting or holding a vigil outside of the prison during his execution. On July 9, 2018, he'd appealed to me for help with the latter:

> Personally speaking, Lisa, if I am to be executed, I would like [to] hear that no one on the side of 'those Against the Death Penalty' will be outside the prison (NSP) where the execution will take place. Let those idiots [who support the death penalty] hang out there alone by themselves during that time and lower their I.Q.'s or show the world what their I.Q. actually is, you know what I mean? Will you please let everyone know that I said this?

I shared his request at the noon vigils, but it created a quandary: how could we protest this wrong while respecting Carey's wishes?

We chatted about Carey's "last statement," which he'd sent me a copy of. In it, he'd written that though the ACLU and his attorney at the Nebraska Commission on Public Advocacy would like to file appeals on his behalf, he'd rather they turn their efforts to his brother, whom he had involved in Van Ness's murder. "I wish they would file a motion for my brother Donald to get him off Parole which he's been on since for-ever it seems like, then that would be perfect for me." He apologized again to his brother ("Please forgive me, Don, somehow"). He also said that he hoped that those "truly" against capital punishment would turn their efforts to those on death row "who claim to be innocent (I can think of four); perhaps it is a fact that they are innocent. Why must they remain there one day longer than all the years they have been there?" He signed the August 2 statement "Carey Dean Moore," and beneath that, "*ex*-Death Row Inmate," with the "ex" written in bolder letters, as if it were a later addition. But Carey said that his longtime friend, Gary Cross, who would witness the execution, felt that Carey had passed up the opportunity to witness to Christian salvation in his final statement. "Let Gary know that that's in our book," I said.

"Yes! Our book. Are you telling people about it?" Carey had told Art, Pastor Bob, Dave, and his brother and sister-in-law, John and Glory. "I'm okay with whatever you decide."

"Some," I answered. "Close friends. Some students. Some of the folks at the vigils. But I'm rather superstitious about my writing. I'm afraid that if I talk about it too soon or with very many people, I'll jinx it."

"Oooh, it's jinxed," he joked, waving his fingers like a magician casting a spell.

"Seriously! It's kind of like waiting to tell people that you're pregnant until after you've gotten through the first trimester when the threat of miscarriage is the greatest. The book is still in its first trimester."

We talked about ordinary things, drifting from Dave to my kids to food to people that we both knew in Nebraskans for Alternatives to the Death Penalty (formerly, Nebraskans Against the Death Penalty), and to the other men on death row. Marco Torres, who had been in the hospital with high blood pressure the last time I'd gone to the death row Bible study, had since had a couple of strokes, even though he was only forty-four. Before Carey was moved to NSP, TSCI officials had allowed him to visit Marco in the hospital so they could tell each other goodbye. Marco was one of the men on death row with whom Carey felt the closest.

I praised him for having gotten a Bible study in place for the others and for finding ways to serve others.

"It sounds . . . it sounds like we're saying goodbye," he said softly.

I teared up.

"Don't cry," he whispered.

I bit my lip and looked away. He had enough on his mind without being reminded of the grief that his death would cause others. Once I felt composed enough to speak without my voice quivering, I said, "We're not saying goodbye yet. I'll be back tomorrow—unless that would take time from your family."

"I can have two visitors at once. If I only have one visitor when you arrive, come on up." His eyes darted to the hallway, where a man carrying Styrofoam food containers was walking toward us. I would have stayed longer, but lunch offered a natural stopping point for our visit. "I'm going to go so you can eat your food while it's hot. Tomorrow," I said as we hugged.

## Sunday, August 12

When I returned on Sunday morning, I planned to stay for no more than fifteen minutes, as I didn't want to wear out my friend. Perhaps it was tiresome or irritating for him to sit across from people who looked sad because they didn't want him to go—or hopeful because there was still time for him to file an appeal. Perhaps our visits were making him second-guess his decision.

The woman at the check-in desk at NSP informed me that Dave was visiting. Of course. Sunday had always been his day to visit. I had never met Dave, but I'd written to him a few times, and once I'd spoken with him by telephone. I had been struck by how alike he and Carey sounded. Earlier in the summer, Carey had sent me a picture of the two of them taken by a photographer in the TSCI visiting room. Though they were twins, the resemblance was slight. Carey was thick, ruddy, and smiling broadly; Dave was taller, thinner, and gaunt. Like Carey, Dave was balding, though with longer hair on the sides, and he had the same light blue eyes. He looked sad and tired. "I tried to get him to smile," Carey said. "Really! But he doesn't like getting his picture taken."

When I entered the room, Dave, who had been sitting at the little table across from Carey, stood up. "Dave was just leaving," Carey said. "But when I heard that you were on your way up, I made him stay."

"Well, I'm glad for that!"

Carey introduced us, and Dave and I shook hands. He seemed uncomfortable and awkward. I complimented him on the recent article in the *Lincoln Journal Star* about his relationship with Carey. He'd told reporter Lori Pilger that it would be a relief if this execution happened. With all of the other dates, he'd had to prepare himself in case it happened. "There's got to be a time to say stop," Dave had said. "I just hope they finally do it, stop messing around and pull the switch, give him a couple of shots or whatever. Do it instead of talking and talking about it." I wondered if he really felt that way, or if he was saying that because it was what his brother wanted and needed to hear ... or both.

I told Dave not to leave on my account, but he did anyway. Then, Carey and I sat down. "I like your dress," he said.

My friend Elly had emailed me on Saturday to say that she'd be wearing black to church the next morning because of the execution. I told her that I would be wearing black after the fourteenth. But on this Sabbath, I wore a kind of festive, Haight-Ashbury look: a dress with a pink, orange, gold, black, and white paisley pattern, and orange earrings. As I'd approached the front desk, I'd remembered my first visit to death row, when I'd wanted to look unremarkable.

"I wanted to look bright and joyous today. But here's a secret," I said leaning in and lowering my voice. "This dress is straight from Goodwill!"

"I can't believe that it's used!" Carey said as he studied my dress. In several of his letters, he had mentioned that when he was a child, he'd worn clothes from the Salvation Army, but they were ragged and dingy.

"I bought used clothes for Ian when he was little. When he was seven, he started complaining, so I bought him new ones—with some good buys every now and then from yard sales."

"That's when kids start noticing?"

I shrugged. "I guess so."

I asked who had visited him here and who else he expected to see. He didn't know if his sisters would come, and he really hoped that Don would. For a reason he didn't know, he had put on his visiting list the name of an Omaha woman with whom he'd been corresponding but had never met. Because she was losing her vision, her husband had driven her to the penitentiary the day before. "You could tell that they were wary about visiting," he said. "They seemed kind of scared. She cried a lot while she was here, but we had a good visit. She's writing to a bunch of guys on death row. I encouraged her and her husband to visit them."

"Maybe you helped her break through something. Now that she's met you, she won't be so afraid to start visiting at TSCI. It takes less time to visit a bunch of people at once at a Bible study than to write a half dozen letters."

"Maybe she could even start a Bible study," he said brightly.

Carey asked about my recent visit with "Ezi." A few years earlier, my daughter, a classical/hip-hop violinist, had started using her middle name, Ezinma (Ezi for short), as her professional name. Carey was doing a better job of calling her by her new name than I was. I told him that I had gotten to see her perform at the launch of the Good4NYC (Five Boroughs, One Hotline for Justice) program while I was visiting. This program offered free legal advice to people in New York City who had been arrested. During the minute between numbers in which she could speak to the audience, rather than promote her forthcoming album, Meredith said, "There's my mom. A friend of our family is being executed on Tuesday in Nebraska. Talk to her about it." And they did. I was so proud of her.

"Those New Yorkers," I said to Carey. "They may not know where Nebraska is, but now some of them know who you are. I talked to several people who are very interested in our book." I thought that he'd be pleased to hear this. Then again, he might be worried that some of the people I'd spoken with at the Good4NYC event would try to stop his execution.

"Well, praise God," he said half-heartedly. Then he brightened. "And thanks to Ezi. Seriously!"

"So, how's Dave taking all of this?"

"He's wondering what he's going to do without my advice."

"Oh, yeah. Dr. Want-to-Be Phil."

He smiled. "I told Dave that I've given him advice for so long that he already knows what I'm going to say. He just has to imagine it. When he misses me, he can read the letters again." Like me, Dave had saved all of the letters that Carey had written him. After his brother's death, Dave would generously offer me access to them. If I had acquired over 320 letters in twenty-three years of correspondence, how many must Dave have amassed in the thirty-eight years that his twin had lived on death row? I thanked Dave but told him that I had more than enough material to work with.

"It's a blessing to have the letters." I paused; I feared tearing up again. "You'll always be alive to me through them." Carey nodded slowly. He seemed touched by my response.

On a shelf next to the table where we sat were bottles of water and individual packages of Oreo and Nutter Butter cookies. Carey opened a package of Oreos, smoothed the wrapper, and divided the six cookies into stacks of two. He was impressed that the staff had refilled his stash and were giving him all the Pepsi he wanted. "Have some," he said. "Everyone likes Oreos."

"I can't tolerate the gluten."

He took a bite and chewed. "Tomorrow, the prison is giving me a last meal. I can have anything I want, so I ordered Pizza Hut."

"What kind of toppings?"

"Hamburger, mushroom, and something else. I ordered strawberry cheesecake and Pepsi. I can have four people, so I invited Dave, Taylor, Bob, and Dave's roommate. I wanted to invite you, but I know you're a vegan or something," he said with a wave of his hand. "So, I invited Rick. He's Dave's roommate, but they're not gay."

I let his last comment go. "I'm a vegetarian with a gluten allergy," I said. But I wished that I weren't. I wanted to be part of the gathering. I wondered if I could come anyway and just eat the cheesecake—all but the crust. But the guest list was set, and the security checks had already been completed.

Carey was happy that he could treat his family to dinner and that they'd be permitted to stay until 11:00 PM. Visiting hours on the day of his execution were from 4:00 to 8:00 AM, and of course, Dave and Taylor would be there early. What would Carey do between the time his family left the dinner and the arrival of his first visitors in the morning? He might be too scared to do anything except, perhaps, pray and read the Bible. Or he might write letters unless he felt that would distract him from his preparations. For his last breakfast, he could order what he wanted from the menu. Normally all he wanted for breakfast was coffee and milk—unless there were eggs. He loved eggs. For his last meal, he wanted a cheese omelet. "They said they could make an omelet with any ingredient but cheese."

"Really? Cheese is pretty standard in an omelet."

"What's hard? Eggs. Cheese. Fold," he said, pantomiming the steps as he talked.

"If they'd let me bring a skillet and a hot plate, we could make one."

Our talk drifted easily to the early years of our friendship when I'd visited him here at NSP. There was so much that I wanted to ask him, as writing a book about someone requires far more information than typical conversational exchanges can provide. *Why were you never able to watch* Dead Man Walking—*or did that change? What was it that you admired about* The Shawshank Redemption? *What happened to the guard who you suspected of poisoning the water jugs that those on death row drank from? Did you, like Karla Faye Tucker, have to remind yourself of what you'd done to end up here because that life seemed so far behind you, or was that always on your mind? Once you asked me what it is that people most like and dislike about me. I thought about that for days. But I don't remember asking you that in return. So, what is it? (I bet I know: your honesty and your honesty, right?) The only positive childhood memory that you've ever told me about was teaching Dave to swim at YDC in Kearney. Please tell me that there are others. Was there anything that you enjoyed about elementary school? Anyone that you had a fond memory of, say, a grandparent or a teacher? Why were you so critical of my efforts to help Ian when he was struggling so in his late teens? When you heard that one of my efforts to help him had backfired, as you predicted, you wrote that you couldn't stop laughing. I was offended, but I let it go. Even so, I still wonder about that uncharacteristic response from you. Maybe you were trying to keep me from making mistakes. Or maybe you were angry or offended or regretful because no one had done for you what I was doing for my son. Are you really ready, mentally and spiritually, for your final departure?* But I thought better of asking such questions now.

One of the stories that I'd have like to have had more details about concerned the time that his father and Dave's girlfriend visited the twins at the "training school" in Kearney. When Mr. Moore took them all into town to eat, the boys told him that they were running away, then stole a car and were gone for a few weeks. Once Carey started running, he loved the escape and couldn't stop. I wanted him to tell me where he and Dave had gone in that hot car and how they'd gotten the food and gas that they needed. I was curious how and where they were caught and how they'd been punished. I was also curious as to why they'd told their father that they were planning their escape. But Carey took the discussion in a different direction.

"I've always had an anger problem," he said. This was a side of him that I'd seen but once: when he'd written to scores of pastors about hosting the death row Bible study but none had been willing to help him. To illustrate his anger problem, Carey launched into a long story about his encounter with an inmate with whom he had responded with anger on at least a couple of occasions. I already knew this story from his letters about this inmate planting shanks in other inmates' cells, which had resulted in several of them being sent to the hole. In this telling, it was more dramatic and detailed. But what I didn't know until he told me the story on death watch was that this inmate had called Carey "sweet meat," a term for homosexuals, in front of others. Carey had responded with angry words. The offender never called him that again. Carey was glad that he'd never had to live in the general population where problems like that were common—a concern he'd expressed many times in the past twenty-three years—and where controlling his anger might have required even more prayer and self-discipline.

Recently, it had occurred to me that I needed him to sign a legal release so that I could publish quotations from the letters that he had sent me. But it was too late for that. I was there as a friend, not as a writer seeking permissions. "Before I forget, is there anything that you want me to be sure to include in our book? Or any hopes for it that you want me to know about?"

He paused. "Nothing I can think of."

"If you do think of anything, let me know tomorrow—or write me a letter."

Amy Miller, the legal director of Nebraska's ACLU and Carey's friend, and his lunch tray arrived at the same time.

I hugged him goodbye and promised to return on Monday.

## Monday, August 13

On the day before the execution, the US Eighth Circuit Court of Appeals denied Fresenius Fabi's appeal and upheld Judge Kopf's decision. Carey could still challenge the untested drug protocol in court; but of course, he wouldn't, and I wasn't going to try to change his mind. Months earlier he had told me that he didn't care if the drugs didn't work as planned—he'd be unconscious. He thought a botched execution might help the other guys on death row, though he didn't specify how.

Now that it was almost certain that nothing would stop the execution, I felt sad, heavy, and hopeless. But I wasn't ready to wear all black. I was happy to be visiting my friend, so I wore a daffodil-yellow shirt, black pants, and gold, fish-shaped earrings.

The weekday guard's pat-down search was much more thorough than that of the weekend guard. My hair was in a bun, as it had been on Saturday, but she took it down and rifled through my hair. "Sorry about this," she said. When I arrived in Carey's room, I commented on the differences between the two, and Carey commiserated. At both NSP and TSCI, he endured a body cavity search before entering and after leaving the visiting room. "Guards are different. Some are fine, but some really get down there and look," he said, pretending to peer into a rectum. "Ack. Disgusting." On death watch, the guards observed him every minute, though they remained just outside of the room when I was there. He put a washcloth over his eyes when he was trying to fall asleep, so he couldn't see them watching him. He appreciated the guard who turned sideways to give him a little privacy when he was showering or using the toilet.

Carey looked tired, but he'd had a wonderful time with his family at the "last supper." His brother John, who had come from his home in New York, came to the dinner in place of Dave's roommate. Carey, who hadn't had Pizza Hut since before coming to prison thirty-eight years ago, said it was every bit as good as he remembered it being. I doubted that I could eat, much less enjoy a meal, if I was going to be executed in a day and a half, but I'd certainly savor the time with my family and my pastor. In a Facebook message, Pastor Bob told me that the guests had stayed past 10:30 PM. At the memorial service on the eighteenth, John would tell us about his brother's generosity. "At his last meal, he offered cheesecake to the guards before he offered it to us! That's just the way he was."

We hadn't had access to a Bible during my earlier visits, but I was glad to see Carey's big, red leather one on the table. Finally, the prison staff had given him his personal possessions. When Carey had awakened at 2:15,

God told him to find a chapter in the Bible that was nothing but the words of Jesus. "What is that?" he asked me.

"Gosh. I don't know. John 3?" I knew that wasn't the right answer as soon as I said it.

"No! John 17. Jesus's prayer for those he was leaving behind." He opened his Bible to that chapter and read it out loud. With the exception of a single framing sentence, which said that Jesus "looked toward heaven and prayed," the entire chapter was one long quotation, one long prayer about Jesus having finished the work he'd been given, his desire for unity among the believers, and his concern for those he was leaving behind. That was Carey's prayer, too.

I, too, had been awakened in the middle of the night. Then, God had led me to the sixty-second Psalm. I repeated the first line ("For God alone my soul waits in silence . . .") over and over until I fell asleep. Carey read that psalm out loud, too.

After he had read John 17 in the wee hours of the morning, he still couldn't go back to sleep, so he wrote five letters. One was to Leona Trauernicht, who had faithfully participated in the death row Bible studies for the past several years. He hadn't expected to write to her again. I was curious who else he'd written to, but he didn't say and I didn't want to be nosy.

After we'd been visiting for about forty minutes, one of the guards stepped in to tell Carey that Amy Miller was at the front desk and wanted to visit him. "Ask her to wait twenty minutes," he told the guard. But because of an elevator problem, she was delayed by almost an hour.

Then, out of the blue, Carey asked me if when I gave birth, I wanted to know what to expect. "I wish that I *had* wanted to know. When I was pregnant with Ian, I went to a class at the hospital about preparing for delivery. It was all about pain and problems. I thought that because of my yoga teaching and practice, I'd hop on the bed, spit out the baby, and hop down. How's that for pride? But my labor had to be induced. It was so long and hard. I screamed—I mean, literally screamed—for painkillers. One reason that Meredith's birth was easier was that I knew what to expect." Then, I realized why he was asking me about this. "They haven't told you, have they?"

"No," he paused for what seemed like a long time. "I imagine . . . I imagine being strapped to the gurney. But that's all I know. You gave birth twice. That's so courageous. What I'm going through is nothing compared to that."

I tried to convince him that facing one's execution with grace and equanimity, as he was, was a far greater challenge than surviving childbirth. "Several hours, maybe a day of labor, and it's over and you have your baby. But what's the point of your suffering? *You* are so courageous. *You* are such an inspiration in how you're facing this." What I couldn't say was that because the combination of drugs that NDCS would be injecting into his veins hadn't been tested, and because this was the state's first execution by lethal injection, we didn't know if it would go smoothly or be bungled and painful.

"Swift and merciful is what I want for you." That's also what I'd told the hospice doctor when he asked what I wanted for my mother as she lay dying.

He nodded. Then he seemed to really hear what I was saying. "Yes, yes," he said emphatically.

We sat in silence. I wondered if he wanted to talk more about the ritual of execution or if I should change the subject. Or maybe we didn't need to say anything.

Then, on the next-to-last morning of Carey's life and the last time I'd see him, something extraordinary happened: I felt moved to tell him stories from our letters, which were fresh on my mind. That summer, I'd reread the 320 that he'd sent me as research for the book that I wanted to write. Some were about events from his life or mine, several of which he'd forgotten. Most were funny or sweet. Each reminded us of the great sweep of time that our friendship encompassed, how much we'd shared, and how much we'd enjoyed knowing each other.

I moved easily from one story to the next—the mouse that had taken up residence on death row; Carey telling me that I could cover the dent that Meredith put in my car as a new driver with a "Bush for President" bumper sticker; the time when Ian visited Carey at NSP and they drank Pepsi and talked about their favorite foods; the staff's confiscating irons and ironing boards and forcing everyone to look like wrinkled slobs; his gallows humor (death was very fast for his victims but very slow for him; he wouldn't believe that his execution had really happened until the day after). It did me good to see him forget his circumstances and laugh with abandon.

"Before my dad died in 2006, he bought me a couple of rhubarb plants at the farmer's market," I said. "Dad and Meredith planted them in the front curb garden. You said that rhubarb was one of your favorites, but it had been so long since you'd eaten it. 'Lord help me!' you wrote."

"That's what I said?" he chuckled.

"I would have brought you a rhubarb pie today, but my ex-husband always told me that if I really liked someone, I shouldn't cook for them." I wondered what the three guards posted outside thought of our hilarity less than twenty-four hours before my friend would be put to death.

"You know, when I met you back in 1995, I never in my wildest dreams thought we'd be friends all these years or that we'd ever be in this position. And what a friendship it . . . is!" I said. I had first reached for the past tense verb but quickly caught myself. "You've taught me a lot about how to be a friend."

"Oh," he said slowly, his typical lead-in to a humble reflection.

"Do you remember that time when you wrote that after much prayer, you'd decided to take me out of your address book, since I was so slow answering your letters and because you expected more of your friends than that?"

He shook his head as he tried to suppress a smile. "I didn't say that."

"Trust me. You did. I've got it in writing."

"Yeah, I do remember. Sorry about that."

"But then you went on to write about a half dozen pages or so about everyday things. I guess you don't hold grudges."

In recent years, it's become increasingly uncommon for a Republican and a Democrat to be friends. But we managed it. "After the 2016 election, you wrote to me that even though you didn't like Trump, you would have voted for him."

"I hated the Clintons," he said matter-of-factly. He'd told me that before. It was the most overtly political comment I'd ever heard from him.

"Well, Clinton wasn't one of my top choices for the Democratic nomination, but . . ." I stopped myself, even though I'm always down for a friendly or a heated political discussion. Surely Carey's refusal to talk politics contributed to the longevity of our friendship. "After you told me that you would have voted for Trump—if you could have voted—you said that you felt bad for me and my side, anyway. I appreciated that." He smiled. I could see that he wasn't going to start talking politics now.

I paused to pull forth another memory. "About fifteen years ago, you were so frustrated with 'Frank' and 'Shawn' and that televangelist they followed. Do you remember that pastor? He was pretty legalistic and had that bizarre theory about the lost tribes of Israel. You wrote me a lot of letters about that."

"Oh, yes," he said with exasperation. "What was the name of that church—that cult?" he waved his hand dismissively. "I had to clean death row with those two, but they wouldn't work on the Sabbath. So, I had to do all that myself. Gosh, that was irritating," he said, shaking his head. But one of those men had been coming to the death row Bible study for many years, due at least in part to Carey's influence—which I reminded him of. "Oh, well," he said softly." "Maybe I had little something to do with that."

"One of the many things I appreciate about you is your ability to help me see what I have to be grateful for. One time I was complaining away about all of the meetings that I had to go to. You commiserated. What a 'heavy weight' I had to bear, you said. I think that you were being sympathetic and sarcastic. Then you offered to go in my place. I felt petty afterwards. I thank you for that," I said. "Then I had fun imagining you at the meeting," I added, "since you don't suffer fools gladly.

"One time I asked you what I should call you. You wrote, 'You can call me Carey, you can call me Dean, you can call me Carey Dean, and you can call me Moore. Just don't call me late for supper.'" I had long called him Carey Dean. His family called him Dean. George called him Carey D. But later, because several people that I knew called him Carey, I did, too.

"I signed my letters according to how people addressed me."

"You always wrote 'Your friend, Carey Dean' on mine, and told me to use my seat belt. After I backed into that mail truck, you always wrote 'Use your seat belt and drive safe.' Your early letters were so exuberant. All those 'PTL's' and 'Hallelujahs' and 'Amen & Amen' and all of those exclamation points. Now, old man, you're more subdued!"

"Praise the Lord!!!" he shouted as he raised his hands overhead.

Even though he already knew the story, I told him how I'd gotten the idea to write a book about our friendship and the letters. When I'd read the headline in the April 4 issue of the *Lincoln Journal Star* that the state was seeking an execution warrant for Carey, I sat down and wept. I knew that he wouldn't fight this most recent attempt to kill him; and because this was an election year, there would be more pressure than usual to execute him. Once I'd dried my eyes, I'd gone to the closet in my spare bedroom, dug out the hundreds of letters that he'd sent me, and began reading them, in order. That was easy. When Meredith was ten or so, she'd needed something to do and I'd tasked her with organizing the letters by year. The yellow sticky notes she'd used to mark each year were still there.

As I read, I soon realized that these letters were too good to keep to myself. But I also knew that my modest, humble friend wouldn't consent to be the subject of a book. When I broached this subject, he said that his life was boring and that he didn't want, need, or deserve attention from so many strangers. But when I told him how much I appreciated what he'd revealed of himself and his circumstances in his letters and asked, "Who writes letters anymore?" he wrote back, "'Who Writes Letters Anymore?' That would make a good title for a book!"

"Hah!" I said, slapping the table. "That's when I knew I had you!"

"Yeah." He paused. "Why do you think you saved all of them?"

"I guess," I stopped to search for the answer. "I guess in some way, I just knew that I'd need them someday."

I hoped then that I could turn Carey's letters into a book. But if I couldn't, all the rereading I'd done over the past several months was worth it at this moment, when I was able to tell him one story after another.

I could see Amy Miller walking down the hall. I figured that the chance of her, or anyone else, convincing Carey to restart his appeals, was less than nothing. The guard who would escort me back to the front desk was waiting by the door. It was time to say goodbye for the last time. I embraced my friend, embraced him again, and left.

## Tuesday, August 14

When I awakened on the morning of the fourteenth, I checked the news to see if a stay had been issued. When I saw that the execution was still on, I panicked. This morning was my last chance to see my friend. Visiting hours were from four to eight. The execution was at ten. If I hurried, I could see him before it was too late. Then I caught myself. No. He had family coming. No. He had preparations. But what was I supposed to do at 6:00 AM on the day of my friend's execution?

If I had been at the penitentiary with the other witnesses to the execution, someone would tell us exactly where to go and what to do. I had come close to being one of them. On July 20, Carey had written: "Here's something to consider as a friend and for your/our book [. . .] would you like to be the third witness at my execution?" When I read that, I wept. I didn't want to watch people kill him; yet, I couldn't refuse my friend's invitation. But there was another letter from Carey. Though dated July 22, it had arrived on the same day as the July 20 letter. "Please forgive me, but I must withdraw asking you if you would like to be my 3rd Witness of my possible execution . . . I am sorry." His twenty-one-year-old niece, Taylor, wanted to be present at the execution with her father, Dave. Carey didn't want his death to be the last thing that his niece remembered of him, but she was insistent. And of course, family had priority over friends. I was relieved not to have to witness the event; however, I couldn't help but worry about how the spectacle would affect this young woman.

I was comforted to know that I wasn't preparing to enter the witness room. But what was I supposed to do here while my friend's life was being taken from him? Even though Carey didn't want anyone protesting his execution, I had considered holding a candle or a sign ("Killing people is always wrong") while standing in the penitentiary parking lot as he was being put to death. But because Carey wasn't fighting the fulfillment of his death sentence, Nebraskans weren't as riled up about this execution as they had been for earlier ones. In fact, most were puzzled and collaborative. I'd heard several people say something to the effect of, "Well, I guess if he wants to die... Let's just get it over with." Perhaps there'd be few who'd even notice a protest.

Still, I had to do something other than sit at home watching the execution coverage on TV. So, at midmorning, I took a long walk in the rain. I kept checking my watch and imagining what Carey was doing—or rather, what was being done to him. But once I started singing—"When peace like a river, descends upon my soul..." and "Healer of our every ill, light of each tomorrow..."—the disturbing thoughts and images lost some of their force. Ian, who only had a few minutes to talk because he was at work, called to see how I was doing. Meredith also called, and we talked for a long time.

When I arrived home after my long, wet walk, I assumed that Carey was dead. It was, after all, well after ten. But when I turned on the television news, I saw that the execution hadn't yet happened. Had something gone wrong? I didn't want to know the gruesome details, but I couldn't turn away from the coverage. At 9:15, Carey had been brought into the execution area shackled at the wrists, ankles, and waist. This image disturbed me more than any other. Why would a man who hadn't filed an appeal since at least 2009, a man who had been a model prisoner and a surrendered Christian, have to be shackled at the waist? There, NSP warden Michele Capps read the death warrant to him. He had sent me a copy of it, so I knew what he heard: that the NDCS would administer to him "an intravenous injection of substance or substances in a sufficient quantity to cause death, as provided by the law."

Though Carey didn't mention the victims in his final statement, he did speak of them in a letter he'd written to the *Lincoln Journal Star* dated July 6. "I'm so sorry for what I had done to these families, even more than anyone can imagine." Were the Helgelands and Van Nesses watching the coverage? Were those on death row watching it together? No. They were probably on lockdown and watching it alone. Were Carey's brothers and sisters watching? Or were they refraining from the moment-by-moment reports and simply awaiting the word that he was gone?

After the warrant was read, Carey was led into the execution chamber. NDCS employees secured him to the gurney, and an employee opened the curtains so that the witnesses could see Carey's body covered with a sheet except for his head and his left arm, from which extended an IV line. I wondered if he'd searched the faces of those gathered for members of the Helgeland and Van Ness families. Later I'd read in the newspaper that Steve and Kenny Helgeland were at the penitentiary during the execution. Kenny had planned to witness the procedure, but in the end, chose not to because he didn't want to be in the same room as the Moore family.

Carey turned his head to the left toward Dave, Taylor, Bob, and Gary and mouthed the words "I love you" several times. I wondered if, as the first drug entered his vein, he silently repeated the same last words as Van Ness had uttered when Carey shot him: "Okay, okay, I quit." No; if Carey had said those words, it would have been years ago, when he stopped appealing. About one minute after the first drug entered his body, he coughed and breathed heavily. His abdomen heaved. The warden checked to see if he was unconscious. One witness claimed that with the administration of each of the four drugs, the IV line jumped. As the drugs entered his vein, his body became still. His face and hands, the only parts of his body that witnesses could see, turned red, then purple. His eyes opened slightly. The executioners closed the curtains between the death chamber and the witness room for fourteen minutes: fourteen minutes when the witnesses weren't allowed to see. These fourteen minutes would be the subject of lawsuits, editorials, and a legislative bill that would require that witnesses, including two state senators, be allowed to observe the entire process. After the coroner pronounced Carey dead at 10:47 AM, a member of the team that had killed him opened the curtain. One witness said that Carey's face had become a mottled, darker purple.

What I wanted at that moment was to be able to talk over the events of the morning with him. I craved his perspective and consolations. But I'd have to make sense of these events myself. I felt some relief that never again would he have to wait for "some sort of outcome." My friend was gone, and I didn't know what to do with myself.

The day passed, though I don't remember what I did until late afternoon. Then, I was ready to be with like-minded people who were also grieving, so I went to a rally at the Capitol hosted by Nebraskans for Alternatives to the Death Penalty. It felt good to be with people I knew from the noon vigils in front of the governor's mansion, many of them old-timers who had also protested Otey's execution decades ago. It felt good to talk to Carey's brother John, who regretted that he hadn't been able to be present at the execution; to speak to Pastor Bob about what he'd witnessed and to hear him address the crowd; to see so many young people protesting this barbaric act. The rally ended, but I didn't want to leave. What was I to do now?

At home, the question remained with me. It followed me as I took a walk, came home, and watered my garden. It enveloped me as I cooked food (I don't remember what), ate, cleaned up the kitchen. Suddenly, I knew. I had to write as many details of our final three meetings as I could remember. Write to turn my friend's suffering to good. Write to end the death penalty. Write to craft a text that would not only save me from despair but bring me peace.

## Wednesday, August 15

My first thought on awakening was that my friend was gone. My second thought was that I had work to do—a final chapter to finish drafting. My day had shape and purpose.

I wrote all morning. I broke for lunch; then, I collected the mail. When I pulled a letter from the mailbox with Carey's handwriting on it, my heart leaped into my throat. And then I laughed. Of course there'd be one more letter.

At 3:00 AM he had written, "I can't sleep though I'm not tired; I keep thinking 'get up and write to some one' and as I'm trying to go to sleep I think of everyone I know and I came across Art and Marco. 'It's them you should write to so get up.'"

Because one inmate can't send a letter directly to another, Carey had to rely on someone else to photocopy and mail this letter to his friends. So, he sent it to me. The beginning of the letter was for me; the rest of it was for them so they'd know what to expect on death watch "in case someone else finds themselves in my shoes either willingly or by force." He told them about the food and accommodations: "Hot Dogs are very small here, buns are the same size, but the food is okay, and there's relish for the Hot Dogs!" He told them about the preparations for his execution: on Saturday, August 12, "they was two group[s] of guys come checking my veins out, creepy! Neck, arms, hands, legs; hey, what about my feet? ☺"

When he was alone after a day filled with visitors on the twelfth, "for a very brief minute, I felt a wave of anxiety (no fear I think) sweep over as I thought about being strapped to the gerney [sic]/bed/whatever and needles poked into me, but after the minute I prayed and felt better. Really, guys. ☺" When I read that, I suspected that perhaps through this letter, Carey was telling me what he thought I should know about death watch for our book, but that he hadn't wanted to tell me in person in case it upset me. He assured Art and Marco that he believed their claims of innocence and that he was praying for them, and for Art's mother. Someday, he'd see them again. I wept when I read these words. I imagined Marco and Art doing the same.

Finally, he signed this letter just as he had the hundreds of others that he'd sent me:

Your friend,
Carey Dean

# Afterword from Carey Dean Moore

When Lisa first asked me if I would like to coauthor her book about our letters to each other throughout the years, frankly I thought she was kidding with me and of course I said no and then she asked me if I'd like to write the preface or an afterward for the book . . . To be honest, I am honored for anything; that would be something indeed!

Throughout my friendship in person and in writing letters to Lisa, so often the conversation was about my longing desire to be executed, to face death (1 Cor 15:53-55*) even on my terms. I've already been on death row nearly for thirty-eight years now, gosh, why go on any longer? I wish I would had been executed back in 2007, I came with[in] four or five days from death's door—it was "my time" I reasoned but God firmly said "No." So here I still am; "in everything, give thanks" (Eph 5:20), "thank You, Lord, for whatever amount of time you'll bless me with while I'm here."

While on the row, I have known many men who joined me on the row—whether they are innocent or guilty . . . Many of these men have received life sentences (without the possibility of parole); a couple had died of drug overdoses and suicides, three men died strapped to the electric chair before it was retired, a couple men either had a heart attack or a tumor of some kind (cancer I think). God knows how much I would like to come to Him!

I have six sisters and five brothers; one of my brothers (Don) I dragged along with me when I murdered the first man—and four or five days later I murdered a second man by myself. I found out recently that Don had thought that I had snitched on him and turned him in when I was arrested, but not in a million years; I have never trusted cops and their mind games! For years, Don hasn't spoken to me or written me; so long ago, I had asked him to forgive me for taking him (fourteen years old at the time) with me in the first murder and he said he had. Four or five days after the first murder, foolishly I convinced myself to murder once more. How stupid I was!

I would like to ask my victim's family to forgive me as well, please forgive me—whether I am executed or not . . . I truly am sorry. I wish I could go back in time for so many reasons, especially for stealing two lives.

Writing to so many, many people over the years has been a lifeline to me, truly—or else I would have wasted away in my life. In fact, I think I was helped a lot as I shared my feelings and thoughts with whom I was writing to when I received execution dates—I was more than able to understand feelings and concerns and maybe worries and fears and God was able to help me accept those feelings, with the help from people I was writing to; quite often throughout the years, I looked at people I was writing to as my personal therapists; and this began years ago when I first came on the row and met my first pen-friend, I shared just a little at a time about the two murders and convincing my fourteen-year-old brother to go along with me on a robbery. Yes, a lot of people was in God's corner, He was telling them what to say and not everyone spoke kind all the time but all spoke with Christian love—love that I desperately needed and ached for. Thank you one and all!!!

Carey Dean Moore

*"For the perishable must clothe itself with the imperishable, and the mortal with immortality. When the perishable has been clothed with the imperishable, and the mortal with immortality, then the saying that is written will come true: 'Death has been swallowed up in victory.'"

# Acknowledgments

This project would not have been possible without the support of the following:

Carey Dean Moore, who trusted me to get his story right.

Meredith Ezinma Ramsay, my daughter and valuable first reader, who spent many, many hours hashing out craft and ethical issues with me;

Ian Knopp, my son, who offered his perspective on many points, a perspective that is especially valuable because often, it's so different from mine;

The late David Moore, who granted me legal permission to publish excerpts from the letters that his brother sent me;

John (Bartley Joseph Moore) and Glory Swiniarski, who gave me support and friendship and who generously shared with me stories about their experiences with Carey and the Moore family;

Julianne Couch, Amy French, Sharon Hatfield, and Astrid Ramsay, whose sharp eyes and insightful critiques at different stages in the writing process made this a far, far better book than I would have produced without them;

Elizabeth Govaerts and Grayson Derrick for their legal and ethical guidance;

The editors at *december magazine* and contest judge Dr. Brittney Cooper, who awarded first prize in the 2020 Curt Johnson Prose Award to my essay, "Death Watch," which was published in the fall/winter 2020 issue;

To everyone at Cascade Books for helping me to bring Carey's story into the world.

# Works Cited and Consulted

## Preface

McPhee, John. "Structure." *New Yorker*. January 14, 2013. https://www.newyorker.com/magazine/2013/01/14/structure.

Zinsser, William. "To Fashion a Text." In *Inventing the Truth: The Art and Craft of Memoir*, edited by Annie Dillard, 141–62. Boston: Houghton Mifflin Harcourt, 1998.

## Prologue

"Clues Sought in Murder." *Omaha World-Herald*, August 22, 1979. https://omaha.com/archive/newsbank/.

"Donald Moore Given Life in Cabbie Slaying." *Omaha World-Herald*, August 15, 1980. https://omaha.com/archive/newsbank/.

Fogarty, James. "Judge Gives Death Ruling in Two Killings." *Omaha World-Herald*, June 20, 1980. https://omaha.com/archive/newsbank/.

"Helgeland Died Three Guns Wounds to Head." *Omaha World-Herald*, August 28, 1979. https://omaha.com/archive/newsbank/

McCoy, Bill. "Shooting of Taxicab Driver Is Second in Last Five Days." *Omaha World-Herald*, August 28, 1979. https://omaha.com/archive/newsbank/.

"Police Probe in Deaths Possible Link in Deaths of Two Cab Drivers." *Omaha World-Herald*, August 28, 1979. https://omaha.com/archive/newsbank/.

## 1. The Challenge

Fagan, Garrett. *The Lure of the Arena: Social Psychology and the Crowd at the Roman Games*. Cambridge: Cambridge University Press, 2011.

Associated Press. "35-Year Hiatus Ends as Nebraska Puts a Killer to Death." *New York Times*, September 3, 1994. https://www.nytimes.com/1994/09/03/us/35-year-hiatus-ends-as-nebraska-puts-a-killer-to-death.html.

State v. Moore, 553 N.W.2d 120 (1996). https://law.justia.com/cases/nebraska/supreme-court/1996/485-2.html.

## 2. The Early Years

Associated Press. "Nebraska Death Row Inmate Switches Places with Twin." *New York Times*, October 5, 1984. https://www.nytimes.com/1984/10/05/us/nebraska-death-row-inmate-switches-places-with-twin.html.

State v. Moore, 553 N.W.2d 120 (1996). https://law.justia.com/cases/nebraska/supreme-court/1996/485-2.

## 3. The Rest of the Story

Beeder, David. "Traffic Arrest More Than Just Routine." *Omaha World-Herald*, August 31, 1979.

"Cabbie Killer Awaits Word Next Month." *Omaha World-Herald*, April 14, 1979. https://omaha.com/archive/newsbank/.

"Court Delays Death Date." *Omaha World-Herald*, July 3, 1980. https://omaha.com/archive/newsbank/.

Duggan, Joe. "38 Years After Killing of Omaha Cabdriver, Time Has Soothed Family's Anger But Not the Pain." *Omaha World-Herald*, February 5, 2018. https://www.omaha.com/news/metro/years-after-killing-of-omaha-cabdriver-time-has-soothed-family/article_7545e2cf-21a4-5a7b-96a1-bf1d7014884d.html.

Fogarty, James. "Brother, Sisters Plead for Slayer's Life." *Omaha World-Herald*, May 22, 1979. https://omaha.com/archive/newsbank/.

———. "Girl Describes 'Shots' in Moore Testimony." *Omaha World-Herald*, April 11, 1980. https://omaha.com/archive/newsbank/.

———. "Guilt of Killing Cabbies: Moore Will Be Sentenced June 20." *Omaha World-Herald*, May 23, 1979. https://omaha.com/archive/newsbank/.

———. "Judges Give Death Ruling in 2 Killings." *Omaha World-Herald*, June 20, 1980. https://omaha.com/archive/newsbank/.

———. "Tapes on Cab Deaths Wrap Up Prosecution." *Omaha World-Herald*, April 12, 1980. https://omaha.com/archive/newsbank/.

———. "Two Tell of Finding Cabby's Body." *Omaha World-Herald*, April 8, 1980. https://omaha.com/archive/newsbank/.

Gullien, Tomas. "Mother Sheds Tears as Hurt Adds to Hurt." *Omaha World-Herald*, August 31, 1979. https://omaha.com/archive/newsbank/.

"Murder's Younger Brother Plead Guilty to Shooting." *Omaha World-Herald*, July 12, 1980. https://omaha.com/archive/newsbank/.

Matteson, Cory. "31 Years into Death Sentence, Moore Says He is Repentant, Tired." *Lincoln Journal Star*, June 27, 2011. https://journalstar.com/news/local/crime-and-courts/years-into-death-sentence-moore-says-he-is-repentant-tired/article_688cd916-8fa9-5dca-aaa5-b8c1902034b5.html.

———. "Victim's Son Says Moore Should Die—or Live—in Obscurity." *Lincoln Journal Star*, June 27, 2011. https://journalstar.com/news/state-and-regional/nebraska/

victim-s-son-says-moore-should-die—-/article_58ea5267-3ee8-50f1-aa16-7829293252f1.html.
Nelson, Andrew J., and Joe Duggan. "'38 Years Has Been Long Enough': Slain Cabdriver's Daughter is Ready for an End to Decades of Waiting." *Omaha World-Herald*, August 9, 2018. https://www.omaha.com/news/crime/years-has-been-long-enough-slain-cabdriver-s-daughter-is/article_b3c11819-b7a1-59c4-9963-e038d9dc9bae.html.
"Panel to Decide Moore Sentence." *Omaha World-Herald*, April 18, 1980. https://omaha.com/archive/newsbank/.
"Two Brothers Are Suspects in Cab Deaths." *Omaha World-Herald*, August 31, 1979. https://omaha.com/archive/newsbank/.
"Two Sought in Cabbie Death." *Omaha World-Herald*, August 23, 1979. https://omaha.com/archive/newsbank/.
Reist, Margaret. "Family Members Remember Men Slain by Moore, Say Legal Wrangling Has Gone on Too Long." *Lincoln Journal Star*, August 5, 2018. https://journalstar.com/news/state-and-regional/nebraska/family-members-remember-men-slain-by-moore-say-legal-wrangling/article_4cc73614-afbe-55be-9c59–3728591a3309.html.
Tysver, Robynn. "Cabdriver Killer Carey Dean Moore Recounted How He Got to Death Row." *Omaha World-Herald,* May 13, 2007. https://www.omaha.com/news/courts/cabdriver-killer-carey-dean-moore-recounted-how-he-got-to/article_c48895ea-dc48-5b14-8b0b4cf01c693dd9.html.

## 4. "What Is Death Row Like?"

"Frakes Announces Bold New Recruitment and Retention Initiatives." Nebraska Department of Correctional Services. October 2, 2017. https://corrections.nebraska.gov/frakes-announces-bold-new-recruitment-and-retention-initiatives-0.
Gonzales, Laurence. *House of Pain*. Fayetteville, AR: University of Arkansas Press, 2013.
Hammel, Paul. "Judge Denies Class-Action Status in ACLU Lawsuit against Nebraska's Corrections Department." *Omaha World-Herald*, June 8, 2020. https://www.omaha.com/news/state_and_regional/judge-denies-class-action-status-in-aclu-lawsuit-against-nebraskas-corrections-department/article_18f9978a-118d-502c-b714-1f59f1df14e7.html.
———. "Nebraska Prisons See Some Improvements, But 'Serious' Staffing Problems Persist, Report Says." *Omaha World-Herald*, September 12, 2018. https://www.omaha.com/news/nebraska/nebraska-prisons-see-some-improvements-but-serious-staffing-problems-persist/article_d65e1cd6-fd1b-5963-8d5f-43ebf1112121.html.
———. "Nebraska's Prisons Are Still Understaffed, Especially Tecumseh." *Omaha World-Herald*, March 5, 2017. https://www.omaha.com/news/nebraska/nebraska-s-prisons-are-still-understaffed-especially-tecumseh/article_afd1baf3-bb3e-5885-87bb-1de66199b76f.html.
Korbernick, Doug. "Summary of the Report on the Death of Terry Berry." State of Nebraska Office of Inspector General of Corrections, August 28, 2017. https://nebraskalegislature.gov/pdf/reports/public_counsel/2017berry.pdf.
Lisak, David, and Sara Beszterczey. "The Cycle of Violence: The Life Histories of 43 Death Row Inmates." *Psychology of Men & Masculinity* 8, no. 2 (2007) 118–28.

"Overcrowding in Nebraska's Prisons Has Led to Constitutional Violations that Endanger the Health, Safety, and Lives of Prisoners and Staff." American Civil Liberties Union, August 16, 2017. https://www.aclu.org/press-releases/overcrowding-nebraskas-prisons-has-led-constitutional-violations-endanger-health?redirect=news/overcrowding-nebraskas-prisons-has-led-constitutional-violations-endanger-health-safety-and.

"Position Statement 54: Death Penalty and People with Mental Illnesses." Mental Health America. https://www.mentalhealthamerica.net/positions/death-penalty.

Young, JoAnne. "ACLU: Expert Reports About Nebraska Prisons 'Quite Scathing.'" Lincoln Journal Star, February 19, 2019. https://journalstar.com/news/state-and-regional/govt-and-politics/aclu-expert-reports-about-nebraska-prisons-quite-scathing/article_514a94cf-a6ca-5af2-8c57-e801c7beab90.html.

## 5. Whispers and Shouts

Coppel, Paula. "Inclusive Christianity." *Unity Magazine*. http://www.unity.org/publications/unity-magazine/inclusive-christianity.

Lamott, Anne. *Traveling Mercies: Some Thoughts on Faith*. New York: Anchor, 2000.

Welch, Gillian, and Dave Rawlings. "Look at Miss Ohio." Track 1 on *Soul Journey*, Acony Records, 2003. Compact disc.

## 6. "A Part of Me Wants to Live, But Most of Me Does Not"

Blume, John H. "Killing the Willing: 'Volunteers,' Suicide and Competency." *Michigan Law Review* 103 (2005) 939–1009. https://repository.law.umich.edu/mlr/vol103/iss5/2.

Chammah, Maurice. "The Volunteer." *The Marshall Project*, January 2018. https://themarshallproject.org.

Cunningham, Mark D., and Mark P. Vigen. "Death Row Inmate Characteristics, Adjustment, and Confinement: A Critical Review of the Literature." *Behavioral Sciences and the Law* 20, no. 1–2 (2002) 191–210. https://files.deathpenaltyinfo.org/legacy/documents/CunninghamDeathRowReview.pdf.

"Executed but Possibly Innocent." Death Penalty Information Center, 2019. https://deathpenaltyinfo.org/policy-issues/innocence/executed-but-possibly-innocent.

"Facts about the Death Penalty." Death Penalty Information Center, February 18, 2021. https://documents.deathpenaltyinfo.org/pdf/FactSheet.pdf.

Gilmore v. Utah, 429. U.S. 1012, 97 S. Ct. 436 (1976).

"Innocence and the Death Penalty." Death Penalty Information Center, 2019. https://deathpenaltyinfo.org/innocence-and-death-penalty.

Mabin, Clarence. "CourtStays Moore Execution." *Lincoln Journal Star*, May 2, 2007. https://journalstar.com/news/local/court-stays-moore-execution/article_576dddab-939f-5623-9bb5-e3f7e0d32dfc.html.

Moore v. Kinney, 320 F.3d 767 (8th Cir. 2003). https://www.courtlistener.com/opinion/3030883/carey-dean-moore-v-michael-l-kinney/.

Pilger, Lori, and Cory Matteson. "Attorney Wants State to Prove Drug Sold to State Legally." *Lincoln Journal Star*, December 23, 2011. https://journalstar.com/news/state-and-regional/govt-and-politics/attorney-wants-state-to-prove-drug-sold-to-state-legally/article_dca0819e-420a-5c58-a421-9e499b1845e5.html.

Rountree, Meredith Martin. "Volunteers for Execution: Directions for Further Research into Grief, Culpability, and Legal Structures." *University of Missouri-Kansas City Law Review* 82, no. 2 (2014) 295–333. http://ssrn.com/abstract=2423868.

Schwartz, Harold I. "Death Row Syndrome and Demoralization: Psychiatric Means to Social Policy Ends." *Journal of the American Academy of Psychiatry and the Law* 33, no. 2 (2005) 153–55.

State v. Moore, 273 Neb. 495, 730 N.W.2d 563 (2007). https://law.justia.com/cases/nebraska/supreme-court/2007/485.html.

Stoddard, Martha. "Nebraska Prisons House an 'Alarming Number' of Inmates in Solitary Confinement, but Reforms Are Promising, National Think Tank Says." *Omaha World-Herald*, November 4, 2016. https://www.omaha.com/news/nebraska/nebraska-prisons-house-alarming-number-of-inmates-in-solitary-confinement/article_4754b4bc-f466-50e1-a216-e88734ee25bc.html.

"USA: Nebraska Looks to First Execution in 14 Years." Amnesty International Website, May 20, 2011. https://www.amnesty.org/en/documents/amr51/043/2011/en/.

## 7. Behind the Headlines

Blest, Paul. "Let's Not Overstate How Good the Criminal Justice Bill Is." *Splinter*, December 19, 2018. https://splinternews.com/lets-not-overstate-how-good-the-criminal-justice-bill-i-1831205306.

Brown, Chuck. "Policy brief—Issues and questions to consider before the budget debate." Open Sky Policy Institute, March 12, 2020. https://www.openskypolicy.org/policy-brief-issues-and-questions-to-consider-before-the-budget-debate?fbclid=IwAR0-H4v6uuFiwrJWe2O4zKLssANX92uj4uHHzYzUlwTFzyBz_SPD2l2-Hck.

Connor, Jill. "Tecumseh Prison's Opening on Hold." *Daily Nebraskan*, November 7, 2001. http://www.dailynebraskan.com/tecumseh-prison-s-opening-on-hold/article_4b1bc150-2392-5121-9dce-a23dd0c610c4.html.

Cordes, Henry J. "Paying the Price: Nebraska Gun Law Helped Spark Nation-leading Prison Growth." *Omaha World-Herald*, Janunary 9, 2022. https://omaha.com/news/state-and-regional/crime-and-courts/paying-the-price-nebraska-gun-law-helped-spark-nation-leading-prison-growth/article_cafde68e-6fb4-11ec-b617-3f9723088c5f.html

"Criminal Justice Facts." The Sentencing Project, 2019. https://www.sentencingproject.org/criminal-justice-facts/.

"Death Sentences in the United States Since 1977." Death Penalty Information Center, 2019. https://deathpenaltyinfo.org/facts-and-research/sentencing-data/death-sentences-in-the-united-states-from-1977-by-state-and-by-year.

Duggan, Joe, and Paul Hammel. "2 Inmates Killed in Disturbance at Tecumseh State Prison." *Omaha World-Herald*, March 3, 2017. https://www.omaha.com/news/nebraska/inmates-killed-in-disturbance-at-tecumseh-state-prison/article_0b574efa-ff85-11e6-a1be-335a27945921.html.

"The Effects of Prison Visitation on Offender Recidivism." Minnesota Department of Corrections, November 2011. https://mn.gov/doc/assets/11-11MNPrisonVisitationStudy_tcm1089-272781.pdf.

Fithian, Tomas. "A Critical Incident Review of the Events Surrounding the Inmate Disturbance on May 10–11, 2015." Nebraska Department of Correctional Services, Tecumseh State Correctional Institution, June 2015. https://bloximages.newyork1.vip.townnews.com/omaha.com/content/tncms/assets/v3/editorial/2/f5/2f5b4d8c-1ea5-11e5-b632-7769b7aeffb0/5591b7a76c338.pdf.

Hammel, Paul. "Inmate Who Killed Tecumseh Cellmate Declines to Fight Death Penalty Arguments." *Omaha World-Herald*, April 20, 2018. https://www.omaha.com/news/courts/inmate-who-killed-tecumseh-cellmate-declines-to-fight-death-penalty/article_7884f75a-0b7c-543a-b94c-8cdff1fc209b.html.

———. "Nebraska Corrections Director Makes Case for New Prison, Drawing Skepticism from Many Senators." January 21, 2021. https://omaha.com/nebraska-corrections-director-makes-case-for-new-prison-drawing-skepticism-from-many-senators/article_426f14ec-5c4f-11eb-880c-a305c239fa40.html.

———. "Nebraska Prisons Chief Says He Withheld Report on Tecumseh Riot for Safety Reasons." *Omaha World-Herald*, December 11, 2018. https://www.omaha.com/news/nebraska/nebraska-prisons-chief-says-he-withheld-report-on-tecumseh-riot/article_64cb12e1-39ee-5758-a155-7648c014f4b5.html.

———. "Tecumseh Inmate Gets Death Penalty; 'May He Rot in the Gates of Hell,' Victim's Grandfather Says." *Omaha World-Herald*, June 4, 2018. https://omaha.com/news/courts/tecumseh-inmate-gets-death-penalty-may-he-rot-in-the/article_ae7e77ff-6d38-5aaa-bc1c-15bd79c84d93.html.

Hammel, Paul, and Joe Duggan. "A 10-hour Battle to Retake the Tecumseh State Prison: Here's How It Unfolded." *Omaha World-Herald*, May 12, 2015. https://www.omaha.com/news/metro/a—hour-battle-to-retake-the-tecumseh-state-prison/article_2421da41-1925-5043-8f1b-a9d810eae925.html.

Hammel, Paul, and Martha Stoddard. "Tecumseh Inmates Dispute State Officials' Report on Riot, Saying It Began As 'Peaceful Protest.'" *Omaha World-Herald*, July 27, 2015. https://www.omaha.com/news/crime/tecumseh-inmates-dispute-state-officials-report-on-riot-saying-it/article_915235ca-32ee-11e5-937a-bf2f3369fdoe.html.

Huddle, Catherine, JoAnne Young, and Casey Welsch. "Inmates Riot at Tecumseh Prison." *Lincoln Journal Star*, May 10, 2015. https://journalstar.com/news/local/crime-and-courts/inmates-riot-at-tecumseh-prison/article_24a22f73-b1da-5b29-9379-f8a17b3d7820.html.

Huling, Tracy. "Building a Prison Economy in Rural America." In *Invisible Punishment: The Collateral Consequences of Mass Imprisonment*, edited by Meda Chesney-Lind and Marc Mauer, 191–213. New York: New, 2002.

Kaba, Fatos, et al. "Solitary Confinement and Risk of Self-Harm Among Jail Inmates." *American Journal of Public Health* 104 (March 2014) 442–47.

Kelly, Bill. "'Coordinated' 2015 Riot Blamed on Existing Conditions at Tecumseh Prison." *NET News*, November 29, 2018. http://netnebraska.org/article/news/1154189/coordinated-2015-riot-blamed-existing-conditions-tecumseh-prison.

———. "Nebraska Prisons Still Housing Two Inmates in Single Occupancy Cells; No Change Expected." *NET News*, December 28, 2018. http://netnebraska.org/article/

news/1133023/nebraska-prisons-still-housing-two-inmates-single-occupancy-cells-no-change.

———. "Withheld Evidence, Judge's Conflict Hinder Case Seeking Prison Riot Damages." *NET News*, November 28, 2018. http://netnebraska.org/article/news/1154123/withheld-evidence-judges-conflict-hinder-case-seeking-prison-riot-damages.

Knapp, Fred. "Update: Two Inmates Killed in Tecumseh Prison Riot Identified." *NET News*, May 12, 2015. http://www.kvnonews.com/2015/05/update-two-inmates-killed-in-tecumseh-prison-riot-identified/.

Lux, Marshall. *Ombudsman's Report: The Mother's Day Riot at the Tecumseh State Correctional Institution May 10, 2015*. http://d1vmz9r13e2j4x.cloudfront.net/NET/misc/40178612.pdf.

Malcolm, Janet. *The Journalist and the Murderer*. New York: Knopf, 1990.

"Mass Incarceration Costs $182 Billion Every Year, Without Adding Much to Public Safety." Equal Justice Initiative, February 16, 2017. https://eji.org/news/mass-incarceration-costs-182-billion-annually/.

Mears, Daniel P., and Jamie Watson. "Towards a Fair and Balanced Assessment of Supermax Prisons." *Justice Quarterly* 23, no. 2 (2006) 232–70.

"Paying the Price for Solitary Confinement." *Prison Legal News*, 2015. https://www.prisonlegalnews.org/news/publications/paying-price-solitary-confinement-aclu-factsheet-2015/.

Pilger, Lori. "'I Was Scared to Death,' Says Ex-Inmate Who Missed Diabetes Meds During Tecumseh Prison Riot." *Lincoln Journal Star*, November 26, 2018. https://journalstar.com/news/local/crime-and-courts/i-was-scared-to-death-says-ex-inmate-who-missed/article_8c2ec348-23ca-5bc8-9641-d171ee784897.html.

Rountree, Meredith Martin. "Volunteers for Execution: Directions for Further Research into Grief, Culpability, and Legal Structures." *University of Missouri-Kansas City Law Review* 82, no. 2 (2014) 295–333. http://ssrn.com/abstract=2423868.

Schlosser, Eric. "The Prison-Industrial Complex." *The Atlantic*, December 1998. https://www.theatlantic.com/magazine/archive/1998/12/the-prison-industrial-complex/304669/.

Schulte, Grant. "Nebraska Prison Proposal Clears Big Hurdle in Legislature." *U.S. News & World Report*, April 20, 2021. https://www.usnews.com/news/best-states/nebraska/articles/2021-04-20/nebraska-prison-proposal-clears-big-hurdle-in-legislature.

Shalev, Sharon. "Solitary." *New Humanist*, January 18, 2011. https://newhumanist.org/uk/Articles/2479/solitary.

Stoddard, Martha. "Nebraska Prisons House 'Alarming Number' of Inmates in Solitary Confinement, But Reforms Are Promising, National Think Tank Says." *Omaha World-Herald*, November 4, 2016. https://www.omaha.com/news/nebraska/nebraska-prisons-house-alarming-number-of-inmates-in-solitary-confinement/article_4754b4bc-f466-50e1-a216-e88734ee25bc.html.

Stullich, Stephanie Morgan. "State and Local Expenditures on Corrections and Education: A Brief from the U.S. Department of Education, Policy and Program Studies Service." Office of Planning, Evaluation and Policy Development (ED), Policy and Program Studies Service, July 2016. https://www2.ed.gov/rschstat/eval/other/expenditures-corrections-education/brief.pdf.

"Tecumseh Wins Prison." *The Grand Island Independent*, May 29, 1998. https://www.theindependent.com/news/tecumseh-wins-prison/article_305baec9-e39f-54cd-abf1-74734c749ecb.html

"Trends in U.S. Corrections." The Sentencing Project, June 22, 2018. https://www.sentencingproject.org/publications/trends-in-u-s-corrections/.

Tsui, Anjali. "Does Solitary Confinement Make Inmates More Likely to Reoffend?" *Frontline*, April 18, 2017. https://www.pbs.org/wgbh/frontline/article/does-solitary-confinement-make-inmates-more-likely-to-reoffend/.

*US News & World Report*. "Unreleased Report: Nebraska Prison Primed for Riot in 2015." November 30, 2018. https://www.usnews.com/news/best-states/nebraska/articles/2018-11-30/unreleased-report-nebraska-prison-primed-for-riot-in-2015.

Young, JoAnne. "Officials Say They're Back in Control at Tecumseh Prison; 2 Inmates Found Dead." *Lincoln Journal Star*, May 11, 2016. https://journalstar.com/news/local/crime-and-courts/officials-say-they-re-back-in-control-at-tecumseh-prison/article_ddbf7fd7-52c1-56fe-acc2-39be4d310b07.html.

———. "Prisons Director Provides Written Testimony on Unreleased Report to Legislative Committee." *Lincoln Journal Star*, December 20, 2018. https://journalstar.com/legislature/prisons-director-provides-written-testimony-on-unreleased-report-to-legislative/article_667fabb2-7bfe-5b49-bd98-c51d51cc1307.html.

## 8. "Just Call Me Dr.-Want-to-Be-Phil"

Chapman, Troy. "Caring Makes Us Human." *NPR's Weekend Edition*, September 28, 2008. https://thisibelieve.org/essay/46556/.

"Increased Transparency for Death Penalty Process Advanced." Unicameral, February 13, 2020. http://update.legislature.ne.gov/wp-content/uploads/2020/02/LB238Pansing Brooks2-13-20a.jpg.

## 9. "Waiting for Some Sort of Outcome"

"Behind the Curtain: Secrecy and the Death Penalty in the United States: Lethal Injection." Death Penalty Information Center, November 20, 2018. https://deathpenaltyinfo.org/facts-and-research/dpic-reports/in-depth/behind-the-curtain-secrecy-and-the-death-penalty-in-the-united-states.

Bush, Randolph, and Steve Mills. "After Death Row, Life Can Be Tough Sentence." *Chicago Tribune*, June 17, 2003. https://www.chicagotribune.com/news/ct-xpm-2003-06-17-0306170220-story.html.

Dilts, Andrew. "Death Penalty Abolition in Neoliberal Times: The SAFE California Act and the Nexus of Savings and Security." In *Death and Other Penalties: Philosophy in a Time of Mass Incarceration*, edited by Geoffrey Adelsberg et al., 106–29. New York: Fordham University Press, 2015.

"Documents Reveal Source of 2018 Execution Drugs." July 23, 2020. The NDCS only released this information because the *Omaha World-Herald*, the *Lincoln Journal Star*, and the ACLU of Nebraska sued prison officials in order to get the information. The case went before the Nebraska Supreme Court, which ordered the department to release the records.

Duggan, Joe. "How Much Does the Death Penalty Cost Nebraska? Economist Stands by His $14.6 Million-Per-Year Figure, Despite Criticism." *Omaha World-Herald*, September 12, 2016. https://www.omaha.com/news/nebraska/how-much-does-the-death-penalty-cost-nebraska-economist-stands/article_81f3c202-801a-5990-9807-baba1682fbba.html.

Eckholm, Eric. "Pfizer Blocks the Use of Its Drugs in Execution." *The New York Times*, May 13, 2016. https://www.nytimes.com/2016/05/14/us/pfizer-execution-drugs-lethal-injection.html.

Goodstein, Laurie, and Sharon Otterman. "Fentanyl Used to Execute Nebraska Inmate, in a First for U.S." *New York Times*, August 14, 2018. https://www.nytimes.com/2018/08/14/us/carey-dean-moore-nebraska-execution-fentanyl.html.

Greenhouse, Linda. "Justices Uphold Lethal Injection Case in Kentucky." *New York Times*, April 17, 2008. https://www.nytimes.com/2008/02/08/us/08cnd-penalty.html.

King, Wayne. "Florida Executes Killer As Plea Fails." *New York Times*, May 26, 1979. https://www.nytimes.com/1979/05/26/archives/florida-executes-killer-as-plea-fails-spenkelink-electrocuted-is.html.

Knapp, Fred. "Executions, Education Discussed in Legislature." *NET News*, March 7, 2019. http://netnebraska.org/article/news/1166729/executions-education-discussed-legislature.

Lester, David and Christine Tartaro. "Suicide on Death Row." *Journal of Forensic Sciences* 47, no. 5 (2002) 1108–11.

Liptak, Adam. "Nebraska Supreme Court Outlaws Electric Chair." *New York Times*, February 8, 2008. https://www.nytimes.com/2008/02/08/us/08cnd-penalty.html.

Lurie, Steven. "The Death Penalty Is Cruel. But So Is Life Without Parole." *New Republic*, June 16, 2015. https://newrepublic.com/article/121943/death-row-crueler-and-more-unusual-penalty-execution.

Mabin, Clarence. "Electrocution Protocol Questioned." *Lincoln Journal Star*, April 20, 2007. https://journalstar.com/news/local/electrocution-protocol-questioned/article_96b72d77-1363-5369-a490-3a37210ee6b7.html.

Matteson, Cory. "Maker of Lethal Injection Drug Wants It Back." *Lincoln Journal Star*, November 29, 2011. https://journalstar.com/news/state-and-regional/govt-and-politics/maker-of-lethal-injection-drug-wants-it-back/article_a127fa70-8d0f-5163-bfbb-e0690bbd3822.html.

O'Brien, Edna. "Waiting." *Los Angeles Times*, September 4, 1994. https://www.latimes.com/archives/la-xpm-1994-09-04-tm-34490-story.html.

O'Hanlon, Kevin. "Company Recalls Nebraska's Lethal Injection Drug." *Lincoln Journal Star*, May 9, 2012. https://journalstar.com/news/state-and-regional/nebraska/company-recalls-nebraska-s-lethal-injection-drug/article_3694f11a-a844-5955-ae7f-a5d9253ed10a.html.

———. "Death Penalty Bill Dies for Year." *Lincoln Journal Star*, May 14, 2013. https://journalstar.com/legislature/death-penalty-bill-dies-for-year/article_4332b549-273d-5667-8016-62d7fb8ef303.html.

"Pfizer's Position on Use of Our Products in Lethal Injections for Capital Punishment." September 2017. https://www.pfizer.com/files/b2b/GlobalPolicy_Paper_Lethal_Injection_Sept_2017.pdf.

148  Works Cited and Consulted

Pilger, Lori, and Cory Matteson. "Attorney Wants State to Prove Drug Sold to State Legally." *Lincoln Journal Star*, December 23, 2011. https://journalstar.com/news/state-and-regional/govt-and-politics/attorney-wants-state-to-prove-drug-sold-to-state-legally/article_dca0819e-420a-5c58-a421-9e499b1845e5.html.

———. "Death Penalty Ballot Challenge Survives Legal Challenge." *Lincoln Journal Star*, July 9, 2016. https://journalstar.com/news/state-and-regional/govt-and-politics/high-court-ricketts-not-a-sponsor-of-death-penalty-referendum/article_dbf336b7-bd6e-5a14-8a5c-c0b239a68d2c.html.

Schulte, Grant. "Nebraska Got Lethal Injection Drugs from Omaha-area Pharmacy." *Washington Post*, July 23, 2020. https://www.washingtonpost,com/health/nebraska-got-lethal-injection-drugs-from-Omaha-area-pharmacy/2020/07/23/49260574-cd44-11ea-99b0-8426e26d203b_story.html.

"State by State Lethal Injection Protocols." Death Penalty Information Center, 2019. https://deathpenaltyinfo.org/state-lethal-injection.

"Timeline: Ernie Chambers' Crusade Against the Death Penalty." *Omaha World-Herald*, May 31, 2015. https://www.omaha.com/news/legislature/timeline-ernie-chambers-crusade-against-the-death-penalty/article_abb1b9ba-c557-53d9-94de-e7575abdca53.html.

Wheeler, Ted. "Nebraska Ordered to Reveal Lethal-injection Secrets." *Courthouse News Service*, May 15, 2020. https://www.courthousenews.com/nebraska-ordered-to-reveal-injection-secrets/.

Williams, David. "Texas' Longest-serving Death Row Inmate to Get New Sentence." CNN, April 16, 2021. https://www.cnn.com/2021/04/16/us/texas-death-row-ruling-trnd/index.html.

Young, JoAnne. "ACLU Argues Death Penalty Case in Supreme Court." *Lincoln Journal Star*, December 5, 2018. https://journalstar.com/legislature/aclu-of-nebraska-argues-death-penalty-case-in-supreme-court/article_2f248ff9-8a4b-5cd7-8bbb-382a32c89d78.html.

———. "Governor Responds to Allegations in Death Penalty Lawsuit." *Lincoln Journal Star*, September 18, 2015. https://journalstar.com/legislature/governor-responds-to-allegations-in-death-penalty-lawsuit/article_fc9ab44f-2389-5420-838a-36bb957d3350.html.

———. "Sentencing Bill, Execution Witness Measure Advanced from Judiciary Committee." *Lincoln Journal Star*, May 23, 2019. https://journalstar.com/legislature/sentencing-bill-execution-witness-measure-advanced-from-judiciary-committee/article_12631e52-4d52-598b-b799-9e1b8f0ce69e.html.

## 10. The Outcome

Berman, Mark. "Nebraska Cleared to Carry Out Country's First Fentanyl Execution, Judge Says." *Washington Post*, August 10, 2018. https://www.washingtonpost.com/news/post-nation/wp/2018/08/10/nebraska-cleared-to-carry-out-countrys-first-fentanyl-execution-judge-says/.

Pilger, Lori. "Brother of Death Row Inmate Carey Dean Moore: 'He Would Just Like to Die.'" *Lincoln Journal Star*, August 5, 2018. https://journalstar.com/news/state-and-regional/nebraska/brother-of-death-row-inmate-carey-dean-moore-he-would/article_444bb976-bf7f-5611-bf13-370c757acfb0.html.

——— . "Carey Dean Moore's Brother, Niece Tell of His Last Hours." *Lincoln Journal Star*, August 14, 2018. https://journalstar.com/news/state-and-regional/nebraska/carey-dean-moore-s-brother-niece-tell-of-his-last/article_c0b3f104-e686-584d-aa25-7f510a54cbed.html.

——— . "State Seeking Execution Warrant: Supreme Court Would Set Date for Moore Execution." *Lincoln Journal Star,* April 4, 2018. https://journalstar.com/news/local/crime-and-courts/nebraska-seeks-execution-date-for-death-row-inmate-carey-dean/article_29abc714-1c7b-5937-9449-5d3e33fb02a4.html.

Reist, Margaret. "Family Members Remember Men Slain by Moore, Say Legal Wrangling Has Gone on Too Long." *Lincoln Journal Star*, August 5, 2018. https://journalstar.com/news/state-and-regional/nebraska/family-members-remember-men-slain-by-moore-say-legal-wrangling/article_4cc73614-afbe-55be-9c59-3728591a3309.

——— . "Victim's Sons at Prison for Execution: 'Let's Let Everyone Rest in Peace.'" *Lincoln Journal Star*, August 14, 2018. https://journalstar.com/news/local/victim-s-sons-at-prison-for-execution-let-s-let/article_a1b53f6d-efd4-5b8c-97c5-1d036258f324.html.

Schulte, Grant. "Drugmaker Seeks to Block Nebraska from Using Execution Drugs." *US News & World Report*, August 8, 2018. https://www.usnews.com/news/us/articles/2018-08-08/drugmaker-seeks-to-block-nebraska-from-using-execution-drugs.

Young, Jo Anne. "Questions Surround What Happened in 14 Minutes Witnesses Were Blocked from Seeing Nebraska Execution." *Lincoln Journal Star*, August 19, 2018. https://journalstar.com/news/state-and-regional/govt-and-politics/questions-surround-what-happened-in-minutes-witnesses-were-blocked-from/article_137b1415-8c67-5f8d-af97-a6b9392b8.

www.ingramcontent.com/pod-product-compliance
Lightning Source LLC
Chambersburg PA
CBHW022121160426
43197CB00009B/1112